INTRODUCTION
TO THE
LOGICAL INVESTIGATIONS

EDMUND HUSSERL

INTRODUCTION TO THE LOGICAL INVESTIGATIONS

A DRAFT OF A *PREFACE* TO THE
LOGICAL INVESTIGATIONS
(1913)

Edited by
EUGEN FINK

Translated with Introductions
by
PHILIP J. BOSSERT
and
CURTIS H. PETERS

MARTINUS NIJHOFF
THE HAGUE
1975

PRINTED IN THE NETHERLANDS

TO

HERBERT SPIEGELBERG

ESTEEMED SCHOLAR, MENTOR, FRIEND

ACKNOWLEDGEMENTS

We would like to express our thanks to H. L. Van Breda, director of the Husserl-Archiv (Louvain), for his approval and encouragement of this project, and to Professor Dr. Gerhart Husserl, Professor Dr. Eugen Fink and the editors of *Tijdschrift voor Philosophie* for their permission to undertake it. We also owe a debt of appreciation to Dr. Karl Schuhmann of the Catholic University of Louvain and to Dr. Elmar Holenstein, Dr. Edi Marbach and Mr. Rudolf Bernet of the Husserl-Archiv (Louvain) for their help in reading the original manuscripts and for putting their excellent knowledge of the Husserl "Nachlass" preserved at the Archives at our disposal. We especially wish to thank Professor Herbert Spiegelberg whose careful and critical reading of our manuscript at an earlier stage resulted in numerous suggestions for its improvement; and, last but not least, our wives, Jane and Pam, for their help in preparing the typescripts.

TABLE OF CONTENTS

TRANSLATORS' INTRODUCTIONS

I. HISTORICAL INTRODUCTION

A. *General Notes*

The selections contained in this volume offer the English speaking philosophical community an important commentary on Edmund Husserl's *Logical Investigations*. Their importance lies first and foremost in the fact that the commentary is Husserl's own: a historical self-interpretation that is seldom found in Husserl's writings — published or unpublished.[1] Perhaps just as important, however, is the fact that these selections present Husserl's view of his first, complete major work[2] in a dual perspective. The two "Author's Abstracts" (*Selbstanzeigen*), published in 1900 and 1901, indicate Husserl's hopes for the freshly printed results of almost a decade of his laborious research and analysis; while in the unpublished "Preface" (*Vorrede*) to the second edition of the *Logical Investigations*, drafted in 1913, Husserl gives an extended commentary on the successes and failures of the first edition of his *Logical Investigations* as well as some of the historical background of their development.

In light of J. N. Findlay's recent translation of the second edition of the *Logische Untersuchungen*, the publication of an English translation of this important commentary by Husserl upon his own work is, in my view, both timely and helpful. Dorion Cairns' faithful translation of Husserl's final, major work on logic,

---

[1] There is a somewhat *shorter* analysis of the ,,task and meaning" of the *Logical Investigations* in Husserl's summer semester lectures of 1925 (cf. *Husserliana IX*, The Hague: Martinus Nijhoff, 1968, pp. 20–45) and also several references back to the first edition of the *Logical Investigations* in *Ideen I, Formale und Transzendentale Logik* and his final unfinished work, *Die Krisis der europäischen Wissenschaften und die transzendentale Phänomenologie*.

[2] Husserl published volume one of his *Philosophie der Arithmetik* in 1891 but never completed volume two (cf. *Husserliana XII*, The Hague: Martinus Nijhoff, 1970).

the *Formale und Transzendentale Logik*[3] of 1929, became available in 1969 shortly before the appearance of Findlay's translation.[4] The translation of the "Preface" published here provides a work from the period of transition between these two major works. Along with Marvin Farber's commentary[5] on the early work and Suzanne Bachelard's on the later work,[6] the development of Husserl's logic and philosophy of logic is almost entirely accessible to the English-speaking reader. The eventual publication of the promised translations of *Erfahrung und Urteil* and *Die Philosophie der Arithmetik* will hopefully soon complete the picture.

B. Historical Notes

After abandoning work in the early 1890's on volume two of *Die Philosophie der Arithmetik* due to problems arising from the inadequacy of the methodological approach employed in those investigations, Husserl spent the remainder of that decade working feverishly on a new methodological approach to the solution of the problems which he had encountered in these earlier analyses. Husserl dates the content of volume one of the *Logical Investigations*, the *Prolegomena to Pure Logic*, to university lectures held in Halle in 1896 but he seems to have been working on the general problematic of the *Investigations* since around 1893/94. The years after 1895 were dedicated almost exclusively to the preparation of the analyses which appear in the second volume of the *Logical Investigations*, so much so as a matter of fact, that according to personal reports of Husserl's wife, Malvine, to H. L. Van Breda, the director of the Husserl Archives in Louvain, Husserl often decided during those years to suspend or cancel his regular university lectures and seminars in order to gain additional time for his work on the *Logical Investigations*.

The first parts of the *Logical Investigations* were published in 1900 while Husserl was still completing his work on the final investigations of volume two. As a result, Husserl apologized in both

[3] *Formal and Transcendental Logic*, Edmund Husserl; trans. Dorion Cairns, The Hague: Martinus Nijhoff, 1969.
[4] *Logical Investigations*, Edmund Husserl, trans. J. N. Findlay, New York: Humanities Press, 1970.
[5] *The Foundations of Phenomenology*, Marvin Farber, Albany, N.Y.: State University of New York Press, 1943.
[6] *A Study of Husserl's Formal and Transcendental Logic*, Suzanne Bachelard, trans. Lester E. Embree, Evanston: Northwestern University Press, 1968.

the "Author's Abstract" to volume two of the *Logical Investigations* and in the "Preface" for the incompleteness of the first edition of his work, for, in spite of extensive and repeated revisions in the manuscripts and even in the printer's proofs, he was unable to incorporate all of the insights he had gained from carrying out the final analyses of the fifth and sixth investigations into the earlier analyses of the "Prolegomena" and the first few investigations of volume two. Husserl himself says in his published preface to the second edition, as well as in the "Preface" published here, that he found his work wanting almost as soon as it was published and took the first opportunity he could find — a 1903 review in the *Archiv für systematische Philosophie XI*, p. 397ff. — to correct some of his more glaring mistakes and self-misunderstandings.[7]

During the years that followed the publication of the first edition of the *Logical Investigations*, Husserl continued his logical analyses. The main problems which occupied him during these years, however, were time-constitution, perception and the ego. His investigations in these areas eventually resulted in a breakthrough sometime during the years 1905 to 1907 in his phenomenological method which he later called "transcendental-phenomenological reduction." After several years of intensive work on this new aspect of his method, he published a first general account of it in 1913 in volume one of his *Ideas*.[8]

At the same time, Husserl also revised the *Logical Investigations* in light of this new breakthrough. During the summer semester of 1908, Husserl had held a series of lectures on "Judgment and Meaning" in which he used the analyses of the first edition of his *Logical Investigations* as a basis for going beyond his earlier position and presenting the new insights and interpretations relevant to this problematic which he had achieved since the

---

[7] Cf. *Logical Investigations*, p. 47. Cf. also Dallas Willard's recent translation of another 1903 book review of Husserl's in which he defends his *Logical Investigations* against criticism it received in a book by Melchior Palágyi entitled *Der Streit der Psychologisten und Formalisten in der modernen Logik* ("A Reply to a Critic of my Refutation of Logical Psychologism" in *The Personalist LIII* (1972), pp. 5-13); and also a report by Husserl on one of his lectures on "Psychological Foundations of Logic" given in Halle on May 2, 1900 (*Zeitschrift für Philosophische Forschung XIII* (1959), pp. 346–48).

[8] Cf. *Husserliana III*, The Hague: Martinus Nijhoff, 1950; translated as *Ideas: A General Introduction to Pure Phenomenology* by W. R. Boyce Gibson, New York: Macmillan, 1931.

initial publication of the *Logical Investigations* in 1900/01. He remarked in these lectures that the *Logical Investigations* were a "good start but still had many weaknesses ... They contain the fundamental material [of his theory of meaning and judgment] but it needs to be developed. We shall use them as a starting point for new considerations of the topic."[9]

The insights Husserl presented to his students in those 1908 lectures — one year after his first lectures on the transcendental-phenomenological reduction[10] — were incorporated to some extent into the revised edition of the *Logical Investigations* which appeared after publication of the *Ideas*. Husserl had originally hoped not to have to publish a revised edition of the *Logical Investigations*. He wanted instead to publish some newer logical analyses that were founded on the original investigations but went beyond them. This new series of systematic investigations on logic carried out within the framework of his method of pure phenomenology would then have made a revised edition of the original analyses unnecessary.[11] And as a matter of fact, Husserl announced a series of lectures for the summer semester of 1912 at Göttingen on the "theory of judgment" which was to be the basis for a publication in this new series of systematic logical investigations. At the last minute, however, he changed his mind and decided to offer a series of lectures on a general introduction to phenomenology. These lectures were then worked up during the fall of 1912 and published in the spring of 1913 as volume one of the *Ideas* in Husserl's yearbook.[12]

As a result of this change in plans, it then became necessary to publish a revised edition of the original *Logical Investigations* and Husserl undertook this project immediately after publication of the *Ideas*. The revised second edition of volume one and volume two, part one (Investigations I through V) of the *Logical Investigations* appeared in late 1913; however, due to the pressing circum-

[9] Cf. page 10 of the typescript under signature F-I-5 in the Husserl "*Nachlass*" in Louvain; cf. also pages 8–10.

[10] Cf. "*Die Idee der Phänomenologie*," *Husserliana II*, The Hague: Martinus Nijhoff, 1958, translated as *The Idea of Phenomenology* by W. P. Alston and G. Nakhnikian, The Hague: Martinus Nijhoff, 1964.

[11] Cf. *Logical Investigations*, p. 44.

[12] *Jahrbuch für Philosophie und phänomenologische Forschung I* (1913), [cf. also fn. 8]. Husserl announces this change in the topic of his lectures and his reasons for doing so at the beginning of the first lecture; cf. Ms. F-I-4, page 4a.

stances of the preparation of this second edition, the revisions in these sections were not as extensive as Husserl had planned. His attempt to do justice to the revision of the important sixth investigation caused it to be delayed repeatedly, first of all due to his constant rewriting and editing of the manuscripts and proofs and then later by the First World War, so that a second edition of volume two, part two — the sixth investigation — did not appear until 1921. By then, Husserl's interests had shifted primarily to the area of genetic phenomenology and, correspondingly, the field of genetic logic. The results of his investigations in this area — beginning around the winter semester 1919/20 in Freiburg when he first lectured on genetic logic — eventually led to the analyses published in *Formale und transzendentale Logik* and *Erfahrung und Urteil*.[13]

Husserl's own copies of the *Logical Investigations* preserved at the Husserl Archives in Louvain indicate that he continued to reread and rework these analyses until very late in his life. As with much of his work — published and unpublished — Husserl was never quite satisfied with the *Logical Investigations*; for, in accomplishing that which he set out to do, he moved beyond that which he had done.

C. Text-critical Notes

The original German texts upon which the translation of the two "Author's Abstracts" are based appeared as "*Selbstanzeigen*" — literally an author's "self-announcement" of his own book — in volumes 24 (1900) and 25 (1901) of *Vierteljahrsschrift für wissenschaftliche Philosophie und Soziologie* (pages 511–12 and 260–63 respectively).[14]

The original text upon which the translation of the "Preface" is

---

[13] *Formale und transzendentale Logik* resulted from Husserl's attempts to write an introduction to the investigations which are now collected under the title *Erfahrung und Urteil*. The former was published in 1929 in Husserl's *Jahrbuch für Philosophie und phänomenologische Forschung* but the latter was only published after his death by his assistant, Ludwig Landgrebe, who had been given the task during the 1930's of editing Husserl's original manuscripts and compiling a book from them; cf. *Briefe an Roman Ingarden* (Den Haag: Martinus Nijhoff, 1968), pp. 62, 97, 99.

[14] The *Vierteljahrsschrift* was at that time the primary organ of German positivism, with such leading German "positivistic" philosophers on its board of editors as Richard Avenarius and Ernst Mach. Up until the *Ideas* Husserl considered himself in the mainstream of positivism and published almost exclusively in the journals representative of this trend.

based appeared in two installments in volume one (1939) of the *Tijdschrift voor Philosophie* (pp. 106–33, 319–39). The origin of this German text is somewhat complicated, however, and requires some explanation.[15]

After finishing the initial revisions of the *Logical Investigations* in 1913, Husserl set about writing a preface for the second edition. The extensive "critical" preface he had in mind, however, proved to be too large a task at that time, and so he composed a shorter, standard preface for the 1913 printing of volumes I and II/1 of the second edition, promising his critical appraisal of the first edition and its critics as an epilogue to the sixth investigation, i.e., the end of volume II/2.[16] The fact that the publication of a second edition of the sixth investigation was delayed until 1921 resulted in this "critical epilogue" being at first delayed and eventually abandoned by Husserl.

A study of the original stenographic manuscripts of the "Preface" contained under signature F-III-1 in the Husserl Archives in Louvain reveals that Husserl had originally composed two separate drafts of a preface — or *"Einführung"* (introduction), as Husserl himself called it. Corresponding to sections 1 through 5 of the present draft of the "Preface" is a manuscript written out in longhand by Husserl and obviously intended in that form for the printers; while corresponding to sections 6 through 12 of the "Preface" is a shorthand manuscript in Husserl's own stenographic style which is divided into seven sections (i.e., section 6 of the present "draft of a Preface" was originally the first section of an earlier draft).

The evolution of the text of the "Preface" from these two, original 1913 manuscripts to the 1939 edition of them by Fink can be reconstructed as follows:

1) Towards the end of September or beginning of October 1913, Husserl worked out several drafts of an "introduction (preface) to the second edition" of his *Logical Investigations*: the stenographic manuscript (corresponding to sections 6–12 of the "Preface")

---

[15] I am very grateful to Dr. Karl Schuhmann of the Catholic University of Louvain who put both his own personal time and his excellent knowledge of the Husserl Archives at my disposal in researching this text. The majority of the information in this section is based on his findings (cf. "Forschungsnotizen über Husserl's 'Entwurf einer "Vorrede" zu den *Logischen Untersuchungen*'" in *Tijdschrift voor Filosofie XXXIV* (1972), pp. 513-524.)

[16] Cf. *Logical Investigations*, p. 50.

represents a rough draft of one such preface which Husserl has explicitly divided into seven sections numbered "1 through 7" while the longhand manuscript (corresponding to sections 1–5 of the "Preface") represents an entirely different draft of the proposed introduction. Which of these two drafts came first is hard to tell, but the longhand draft is probably a transcription by Husserl himself based upon an earlier stenographic draft, since this was usually the manner in which he worked. Pressed for time, Husserl eventually abandoned this project as a preface and decided to rework it later as an epilogue. He did, however, incorporate certain aspects of these early drafts of the longer "critical preface" into the shorter preface which was actually published in 1913 (a comparison of the "Preface" here translated and the actual preface to the 2nd edition — Findley, pp. 43–50 — reveals numerous similarities).

2) Some time between 1915 and 1917, in connection with his repeated attempts to get the sixth investigation ready for publication Husserl had Edith Stein, his assistant at that time, transcribe his original drafts of the "Preface." Since she usually transcribed Husserl's stenographic manuscripts only into longhand — she could not type — she probably transcribed only Husserl's shorthand draft — she has a note at the beginning of the stenographic draft to this effect — and then added it to Husserl's own 1913 longhand draft (sections 1–5), thereby producing a single draft of one long preface from the two shorter ones. It is possible that she herself provided the transition passages which linked the two shorter drafts — there are passages in Fink's 1939 edition which are missing from Husserl's original 1913 drafts — or that Husserl himself added them to Stein's transcriptions in order to form the single text. Dr. Schuhmann dates Stein's longhand draft around March or April of 1917 — primarily on the basis of her letters to Roman Ingarden.[17] Stein's transcription however has been lost.

3) In June 1924, Husserl had Ludwig Landgrebe make another transcription of the drafts of the "Preface"; Landgrebe possibly used Stein's longhand transcription as a basis for his own typescript — which notes on other typescripts in the Archives indicate was often the case — or he may have worked directly with Husserl's

---

[17] Cf. *Phil. and Pheno. Research* (1962), p. 166.

original 1913 drafts. Landgrebe's notes at the top of the first pages of both Husserl's longhand draft (sections 1–5) and his shorthand draft (sections 6–12) indicate however that Landgrebe completely transcribed both 1913 drafts of the "Preface" once again in June of 1924.

Why Husserl had Landgrebe transcribe these drafts of a preface to the second edition of the *Logical Investigations* again in 1924 — 3 years after the 6th investigation had been republished (without the promised epilogue) — is puzzling. Perhaps Husserl decided to try once more to publish it, only to abandon the project once again. There are however some passages in Husserl's "Kant oration"[18] of June 16, 1924, very similar to several in the "Preface" which suggest that Husserl may have been reworking the drafts of the "Preface" once again around this time and may have added some of the changes which are present in the 1939 text but missing from his original 1913 drafts.

4) In 1938 Father H. L. Van Breda brought Landgrebe's typed transcript of the draft of the "Preface" from Freiburg to Louvain as part of the Husserl *"Nachlass"* he was able to rescue from Germany. In 1939, he asked Eugen Fink to edit this typescript for publication in volume one of a new journal, *Tijdschrift voor Philosophie*, which was being founded in Louvain. Fink agreed and upon receipt of the transcript from Father Van Breda, edited the text, adding the section headings and a brief editorial preface. This text was then sent to the printer and published in two installments in the journal (Landgrebe's 1924 typescript also seems to have been lost sometime during this process).

These notes on the rather complicated evolution of the German text on which the translation is based are, in my opinion, necessary to reveal the actual circumstances surrounding the "Preface." The text is definitely Husserl's and stems almost entirely from 1913 — a comparison with Husserl's original stenographic and longhand manuscripts verifies this — but between the time Husserl originally drafted it (1913) and the time it was first published (1939) this same text was handled by three of Husserl's assistants (Stein, Landgrebe and Fink) in their transcriptional and editorial capacities as his assistants and most likely reworked one or more times to some extent by Husserl

[18] Cf. *Husserliana VII*, p. 238ff.

himself. Such text-critical information, which will undoubtedly also accompany the eventual publication of the German text in a critical *Husserliana* edition, must be provided in order to enable the critical reader to achieve an accurate understanding of both the text and, in the long run, of Husserl himself.

PHILIP J. BOSSERT
Hawaii Loa College
Oahu, Hawaii

A. Notes on the Purpose of the "Preface"

Husserl's purpose in writing the "Preface" was to "introduce" the *Logical Investigations* in a way that would make the methodology and the content of his work more accessible to the reader.[1] Husserl himself indicates his purpose:

> Keeping in mind the motifs which determined the development of my thought, I want to try to clear up some of the most important misinterpretations [*Missdeutungen*] and thereby to enable the reader, free from them, to take an open stance toward the actual content of the work. It is, therefore, not my intention to go into the innumerable objections [*Einwände*] for the purpose of giving a detailed rebuttal.[2]

In the "Preface" Husserl also remarks that at the time of the publication of the *Logical Investigations*,

> a preface or an introductory chapter ought to have prepared the reader historically and topically and ought to have warned him of all of the misinterpretations which were suggested by the prevailing trends of thought.[3]

It is not Husserl's intent to treat specific "objections" to the various investigations he had carried out. He himself had such objections, and he had had some reservations about the *Logical Investigations* already at the time of its publication.[4] The "Preface" contains, in general, neither replies to specific objec-

---

[1] In the same way this "introduction to an introduction" is to make the thought of Husserl's "Preface" more accessible. One might wonder whether an introduction should itself be the subject of an introduction. The only justification this one receives is that the span in time, language, style and thoughtworld which separates us from Husserl's writing can make access to his views and arguments difficult.

[2] "Preface," p. 19.

[3] *Ibid.*, p. 16.

[4] Cf. the "Historical Introduction."

tions nor attempts to improve upon his earlier views.[5] The *Logical Investigations* is allowed to stand on its own merits.

And it becomes apparent as Husserl proceeds that his desire to clear up "misinterpretations" is not so much one of correcting mistaken interpretations (interpretations that embody fundamental errors) as it is one of ruling out misguided interpretations (interpretations that cannot possibly succeed because they are based upon entirely wrong-headed approaches to the *Investigations*). Such "misinterpretations" are serious because they virtually preclude any possibility of understanding the *Logical Investigations* in particular or phenomenology in general.

One of the values of the "Preface" lies in its specification of those positions which lead to misguided interpretations. In this respect the "Preface" has much in common with his earlier essay (1911) entitled *"Philosophie als strenge Wissenschaft,"*[6] in which Husserl argued that phenomenology alone could bring philosophy to its proper scientific state and that naturalism and historicism were both misguided approaches to philosophical questions because they both prohibited philosophy from becoming a rigorous science.[7]

Because Husserl saw the misinterpretations of the *Logical Investigations* to be closely related to mistaken ideas about the philosophical ancestry of the thoughts presented in the book, Husserl includes as part of his broader purpose both clarification of what he had and had not adopted from other philosophers of his time as well as a presentation of the general historical development of the major ideas developed in the *Logical Investigations*.

B. *Notes on the Content of the "Preface"*

The following views are treated by Husserl in the "Preface"[8] as

---

[5] The latter was, of course, a purpose partially carried out in the second edition of the *Investigations*.

[6] Translated as "Philosophy as a Rigorous Science" in Edmund Husserl, *Phenomenology and the Crisis of Philosophy*, trans. Quentin Lauer, New York: Harper & Row, 1965.

[7] By "naturalism" Husserl has in mind attempts to ground knowledge upon uncritical natural science and especially upon experimental psychology. The reference to "historicism" is directed primarily against Dilthey's position. The "misinterpretations" singled out in the "Preface" will be discussed below in the section entitled "Notes on the Content of the 'Preface'."

[8] In several cases these views are treated twice in the "Preface." There is some indication in the numbering of the sections in the manuscript that sections 6–12 were once separate from or another draft of sections 1–5, and this would account for the

the bases for several misguided interpretations of the *Logical Investigations*:

> 1. There are only two theoretical positions which can account for our knowledge in the mathematical-logical sphere: psychologism and transcendental idealism.
> 2. Any philosophical position which seems to involve "Platonism" or "scholastic realism" is patently wrong.
> 3. The boundaries of the logical realm have been clearly and finally delineated in traditional logic.
> 4. Phenomenology is the "analysis of meanings."
> 5. Logicism is a basic threat to psychology.

One might list as a separate point (although Husserl considers it to be intertwined basically with those listed above):

> 6. A work may be understood through tracing the historical ancestry of its thoughts.

Mention will be made of a few of Husserl's concerns relevant to these misinterpretations.

> 1. There are only two theoretical positions which can account for our knowledge in the mathematical-logical sphere: psychologism and transcendental idealism.

This misguided view has led some readers to set the *Logical Investigations* aside after reading the "Prolegomena" thinking that the whole book is simply an attack upon psychologism, it has led some to think that Husserl has regressed into psychologism in the actual investigations, it has led interpreters to view his book variously as an expression of impure idealism or impure psychologism, and it has led others (e.g., Natorp) to view the book as incomplete in its attempt to resolve the conflicts between the psychological and the logical motifs.

Husserl was clearly opposed to psychologism. The proponent of psychologism[9] claims that the essential theoretical basis of normative logic lies in psychology. Logic in this view is a subdivision or branch of psychology. Introspection is the only appropriate

---

duplication. Cf. the translator's footnote at the end of section 5 of the "Preface" and the "Historical Introduction."

[9] The movement goes back to the works of Jakob F. Fries (*System der Metaphysik*, 1924) and Friedrich E. Beneke (*Die Philosophie in ihrem Verhältnis zur Erfahrung, zur Spekulation, und zum Leben*, 1833). Their proposal was that introspection was the only tool at philosophy's disposal. John Stuart Mill, (*A System of Logic*, 1843, and *Examination of Sir William Hamilton's Philosophy*, 1865) and Theodor Lipps (*Grundzüge der Logik*, 1893) applied psychologism specifically to logic.

method for developing the principles of logic. Husserl rejects the position in part because it distorts the phenomena of the logical realm by treating them as though they were in the empirical realm and because it does not yield the universally valid truth which is necessary if philosophy is to become a genuine science and if it is to enable other disciplines to become phenomenologically clarified sciences.

But Husserl was not developing a transcendental idealism. He wished to investigate the intuitive experience of phenomena in the mathematical-logical sphere *as they presented themselves*, i.e., without forcing them into either of the two accepted interpretations.

Those who fell victim to this first misinterpretation were not only unable to examine mathematical-logical phenomena without interpreting them according to pre-established types — they were unable to examine Husserl's phenomenological approach without slotting it into a preestablished position (or without criticizing it severely for not fitting neatly into such a position). They were unable to see that Husserl is interested above all else in being honest and open in the intuitive experience of the phenomena — even if that means that he cannot fit it into the accepted views or develop a complete, finished view of his own.

> 2. Any philosophical position which seems to involve "Platonism" or "scholastic realism" is patently wrong.

This misguided view has led readers to set the *Logical Investigations* aside as soon as it appears that Husserl will hypostasize entities in the ideal realm.

But it is clear that Husserl's honest and open approach to the phenomena requires that he build upon what he finds — and even such pejorative epithets as "Platonism" and "scholastic realism" will not concern him if his intuitive experience of the phenomena leads him in the direction of those positions. Indeed, Husserl claims to have an appreciation for "Platonism."

But, in fact, Husserl denies that either label can be applied appropriately to his views. The objects which he has examined do not admit of such simplistic categorization.

Those who fell victim to the second misinterpretation were unable to view the phenomena as they presented themselves because they were prejudiced to discount anything that looked like a Platonic ideal or a real entity as described in scholasticism — and they were unable to examine Husserl's phenomenological approach openly for the same reason. Husserl wishes to maintain that "scientific" examination of phenomena is utterly impossible as long as one uses or fears convenient positions and epithets. The final criterion of all knowledge must be simply and only what one experiences in the phenomena.

> 3. The boundaries of the logical realm have been clearly and finally delineated in traditional logic.

Husserl does not so much present and analyze this misguided view as give his own view of the dimensions of the logical realm. The misinterpretation apparently misunderstood and rejected the *Logical Investigations* because the misguided view of logic as a more limited realm precluded a vision of the full scope and import of Husserl's labors. It was either missed or rejected that the *Logical Investigations* were a first step toward establishing universally valid truth in philosophy and toward putting the sciences on a new foundation. Husserl was not interested merely in mathematics or in logic in any narrow sense; he wished to develop a new understanding of the entire mathematical-logical realm, i.e., the entire sphere of the *a priori*, by being more faithful to the intuitive experience of all of the phenomena in that realm.

> 4. Phenomenology is the "analysis of meanings."

By trying to capture phenomenology in this handy slogan, this misguided interpretation greatly reduces the scope and the import of phenomenology. Husserl admits that "analysis of meanings" is, in a certain sense, included in phenomenology, but this slogan (and, presumably, any other slogan) is incapable of capturing the richness of the phenomenological method for understanding any of the many types of objects we experience.

By trying to pigeonhole phenomenology in this handy phrase, the interpreter has prematurely made a judgment about all of phenomenology — before he has painstakingly, honestly, and openly examined phenomenology in all of its dimensions. It is to be expected that such a person will not be able to view openly and carefully the phenomena examined in the *Logical Investigations* either.

5. Logicism is a basic threat to psychology.

Here is again a case where the use of an epithet stands behind a misguided interpretation. By logicism Husserl (following Wundt) means the attempt to understand the association among appearances through logical reflection. The concern expressed in the misinterpretation is that psychology will be subsumed under the discipline of logic. (Logicism is thus seen as the complete antithesis to psychologism.)

But this concern and the tendency to judge something apart from the careful examination of that thing itself rule out the possibility of understanding the *Logical Investigations* and the phenomena explored in it. They have blinded the interpreter, Husserl says, to the fact that his position is not logicism — it is rather a move in the direction toward developing a phenomenologically clarified logic.

6. A work may be understood through tracing the historical ancestry of its thoughts.

Husserl treats this basically as a contributor to several of the misinterpretations already touched upon. It leads the interpreter to stop short of a full, open examination of a work on its own merits. Furthermore, it tends to evade the question of what is true in a work. And, as Husserl indicates is true of the *Logical Investigations*, it can lead to premature and mistaken notions about the historical dependencies themselves.

Husserl's "Preface" is an appeal for a "fair hearing" for the *Logical Investigations*, but it is much more than that. It is an appeal for the adoption of the attitudes which are so basic to the phenomenological method itself. It is an attempt to show how the lack of those attitudes makes a sound understanding even of a book about phenomenology impossible.

The misinterpretations which are criticized in the "Preface" are in some cases historically dated, but the same predispositions responsible for those misinterpretations will be as effective today as they were 70 years ago in precluding both the comprehension of new ideas and the open, careful consideration of our experience of phenomena. Distinctions into which phenomena are forced, pre-established categories, labels, slogans, the concern that new

ideas and phenomena be made to fit in with the accepted theories
of the day, and the search for the historical ancestries of ideas will
still rule out the understanding or use of phenomenology, and they
will still stand in the way of the scientific development of philosophy and of other disciplines.

In the course of revealing some of the sources of the above misinterpretations, Husserl developed substantive claims which are
of interest in their own right — philosophically and historically.
I have singled out a few of those special claims for brief comment.

> 1. The empirical and psychological (mental acts, etc.) must not be
> confused with the purely logical (logical and mathematical concepts,
> etc.).

It was part of Husserl's attack upon psychologism to show that
mathematical and logical concepts could not possibly be understood in empirical, psychological terms, but he did not wish to
subsume the psychological under the ideal, either. The second
volume of the *Investigations* goes beyond the critique of psychologism to explore the more exact nature of relevant phenomena, and
it does so without a commitment to psychologism or to a simplistic
anti-psychologism.

> 2. Fundamental epistemological problems can only be solved by
> reworking them until the objects of thought can be intuitively ex-
> perienced in a direct way.

Husserl's investigations were primarily attempts to examine
directly the basic phenomena of mathematico-logical thinking
and to determine thereby the bases for the judgments we make in
this sphere. Husserl used the language of vision to express himself
on this point. He claimed to "see" mathematico-logical concepts
with the same clarity he could see a table. The similarities and
differences between natural vision and the intuitive experiencing
of logical concepts are not explored, however.

> 3. Direct experience (vision is the model) is the ultimate test for all
> knowledge.

In speaking about the perception of a table, Husserl himself
says, "One cannot philosophize away anything thus seen; it is in
all proper philosophizing the ultimate standard."[10] And he finds

[10] "Preface," p. 27.

no reason for denying the validity of this criterion also in the "ideal" realm. The intuitive experiencing of "ideal objects" should not have to conform to what we might think about the ideal realm; on the contrary, our thoughts about this realm should conform to the intuitive experience. In the ideal realm as well as in the empirical theories, accepted views should never take precedence over direct experience. The very principle of *consistency* itself must take second place to ruthless honesty in admitting and reporting what one observes.

4. Admission of "ideal-objects" in the epistemological sphere is *not* tantamount to metaphysical Platonic hypostatization.

Husserl readily admits that he does not hold the "accepted" view on "ideals" and "givens," but he resolutely denies that he is promoting, knowingly or unknowingly, a metaphysical hypostatization. He refuses to allow a metaphysical position to affect his intuitive experiencing in the ideal realm. The unresolved problems and the special nature of the objects in the ideal realm cannot be ignored or wished away through the adoption of a metaphysical position. Husserl, much like the child in "The Emperor's New Clothes," thought that the previously held theories about mathematical and logical judgments all left the basic issues as naked and unresolved as ever.

5. Pure logic is *mathesis universalis*. The philosophy of pure logic is the investigation of our consciousness of the realm of *mathesis universalis*.

Husserl means by *mathesis universalis* the entire realm of the analytic *a priori*; the *Logical Investigations* is about much more than logic in the traditional sense. The philosophy of pure logic only begins when one seeks to understand our consciousness of the concepts and truths of *mathesis universalis*. The philosophy of pure logic would provide a "theory of mathematical knowledge" giving it its "possible true meaning" and its "right to validity." The results of the phenomenological investigations of the ideal realm are the basis for the phenomenological clarification of other disciplines.

6. Transcendental phenomenology provides the "first philosophy."

If we describe "first philosophy" as the "universal fundamental-science," then, according to Husserl, the obvious path to it is the path of transcendental phenomenology. Our consciousness of the basic concepts and truths of the positive sciences is in need of an examination and determination which only phenomenology can provide. Phenomenology can bring philosophy to universally valid truth, and it will lead to a body of knowledge which will be foundational for *all* science and knowledge and which will overcome the division between science and philosophy.

> 7. Phenomenology is the analysis of essences connected with any form of consciousness.

We have seen why Husserl was not happy with any attempt to summarize his philosophy in a few words, but he was particularly perplexed by the characterization of phenomenology as the analysis of the meanings of words. He views the subject matter for his investigations as a sphere broader than the "meanings of words" — he would include perception, fantasy, and image-conceptualization, for example. Phenomenology examines our intuitive experience of the essences in any act of consciousness whatsoever.

C. Notes on the Value of the "Preface"

The value of the "Preface" is acknowledged by such scholars as Fink, Van Breda, Spiegelberg and Farber. Farber writes, "It is a brilliantly formulated document, and is of great value for the understanding of his philosophical development, as well as of the nature and program of phenomenology."[11]

The value of the "Preface" lies in the several important functions that it fulfills. It is of obvious importance in showing how Husserl himself thought some of his views differed from those of his contemporaries and immediate predecessors. It presents several misguided approaches to the *Logical Investigations* which, according to Husserl himself, ruled out the possibility of understanding the book and phenomenology. It shows the essential unity and continuity which Husserl saw in his philosophy from the *Logical Investigations* through the *Ideas* and related works. It highlights what Husserl later viewed as the most important themes of the *Logical Investigations* and offers some indication of

---

[11] Farber, Marvin, *The Foundation of Phenomenology*, 3rd. ed., Albany, New York: State University of New York Press, 1968, p. 200.

what he came to see as its shortcomings. And finally it provides an introduction to the *Logical Investigations* by making the methodology and several of the themes in that work more accessible — and perhaps it provides a concise introduction to Husserl's phenomenology in general for much the same reason.

CURTIS H. PETERS
Concordia Senior College
Fort Wayne, Indiana

III. TRANSLATION NOTES

The main texts of the English translations which follow are the result of an attempt to render as faithfully as possible the sense and the style of the original German texts described in section I.C of these remarks. For the sake of clarity, we have in some cases inserted the original German term — in brackets — into the text after an English term whose sense may be ambiguous. We have also employed this same means for establishing — at their first occurrence in the text — a correlation between the key German terms of Husserl's philosophical vocabulary — such as *Bedeutung, Anschauung*, etc. — and the English terms we have used to translate them. The additions to the text which appear in parentheses stem from either Husserl himself or from his assistants in their transcriptions of Husserl's original text (cf. text-critical notes in section C of these remarks).

Those deviations from the German texts which have resulted from our attempts to correct printer's errors and, in some few cases, obvious sense-distorting transcriptional errors have been explicitly indicated in footnotes to the main text.

For the sake of continuity, we have tried to take into account both J. N. Findley's rendering of key terms in his translation of Husserl's *Logische Untersuchungen* and also Dorion Cairns' rendering of key terminology in his translation of the *Formale und Transzendentale Logik*. However, these two excellent translators are not always in agreement in their rendering of Husserl's often difficult vocabulary nor are we always in agreement with them.

Page numbers of the original editions of the texts here translated have been indicated in brackets in the margins of the text of the translation to aid the reader who wishes to refer to the original German text.

THE AUTHOR'S ABSTRACTS

1900/01

AUTHOR'S ABSTRACT TO VOLUME ONE

IN

Vierteljahrsschrift für wissenschaftliche Philosophie
Vol. 24 (1900), pp. 511–12

Husserl, Edmund, *Logical Investigations*, Part One: Prolegom- ⟨511⟩
ena to Pure Logic. Halle: Max Niemeyer, 1900[1]. XII and 257
pages.

The "Prolegomena to Pure Logic," which comprise[s] the introductory part of the *Logical Investigations*, seek[s] to blaze a new
trail in the conception and treatment of logic. It attempt[s] to
show that the exclusively psychological grounding of logic, to
which our age ascribes so great a value, rests on a confusion of
essentially distinct classes of problems, on presuppositions erro-
neous in principle concerning the character and the goals of the
two sciences which are involved here — empirical psychology and
pure logic. In detailed analyses, the epistemological and especially
the sceptical complications which are necessarily indigenous to a
psychologistic logic are revealed and, at the same time, it is also
proved that the inadequate treatment of the hitherto existing
logic, its lack of clarity and theoretical rigor are due to a mis-
conception of the most essential foundations and problems. Directed against the dominant psychologism, the "Prolegomena"
thus seek[s] to revive the idea of a pure logic but, in addition, also
to give it a new shape. It result[s] in the demarcation of a theoretical science independent of all psychology and factual science,
a science which embraces within its natural boundaries the entirety of pure arithmetic and theory of manifolds. The relation of this
new science to *logic as a methodology*, as a technique of scientific ⟨512⟩
cognition whose justification remains, of course, unaffected, is
conceived in analogy to the relationship of pure geometry to

---

[1] Because a number of copies sent out in December, 1899, and in July, 1900, named
Veit & Co. in Leipzig as the publisher, I want here to expressly indicate the change in
publishing houses which occurred before the book was published. [Husserl's footnote]

surveying. The most essential theoretical foundations of logical technique are not to be found in the psychology of knowledge — although this too comes under consideration — but in pure logic.

This pure logic is nothing less than a simple restoration of traditional formal logic or also of the pure logic of the Kantian and Herbartian schools. Although the author considers these latter and not yet forgotten efforts as valuable beginnings, they are, in his conviction, lacking in sufficient clarity concerning the goals and limits of the disciplines in question; they still remain in uncertain vacillation between theoretical and practical, psychological and purely ideal tendencies.

Pure logic is the scientific system of ideal laws and theories which are purely grounded in the *sense* [*Sinn*][2] of the ideal categories of meaning [*Bedeutung*];[2] that is, in the fundamental concepts which are common to all sciences because they determine in the most universal way what makes sciences objectively sciences at all: namely, unity of theory. In this sense, pure logic is the science of the ideal "conditions of the possibility" of science generally, or of the ideal constituents of the idea of theory.

An *adequate* clarification of pure logic — i.e., a clarification of its essential concepts and theories, of its relationship to all other sciences, and of the way in which it regulates them — demands very radical phenomenological (that is, purely descriptive-psychological and not genetic-psychological) and epistemological investigations. One might say that this task of an epistemological clarification of logic coincides for the most part with the critical clarification of thinking and knowing in general, i.e., with epistemology itself. In Part II, there will then follow specific phenomenological and epistemological investigations which seek to solve the main problems of a clarification of logic and logical thinking.

The prolegomena have been in print since the end of November 1899, and, due to unforeseen circumstances, are being distributed very late. The second part is in press and will be distributed this winter.

---

[2] "*Sinn*" and "*Bedeutung*" can, in some cases, both be rendered as "meaning" but Husserl almost always has a distinction in mind when he uses these two words, especially when they occur together as above (cf. also p. 5). Thus, we have always translated "*Sinn*" as "sense" and "*Bedeutung*" as "meaning" to indicate Husserl's choice of terminology [Trans. note].

AUTHOR'S ABSTRACT TO VOLUME TWO

IN

Vierteljahrsschrift für wissenschaftliche Philosophie und Soziologie,[1] Vol. 25 (1901), pp. 260–63.

Husserl, Edmund, *Logical Investigations*, Part Two: Investi- <260> gations towards a Phenomenology and Theory of Knowledge. Halle: Max Niemeyer, 1901, XVI and 718 pages.

This volume contains six interrelated essays on phenomenological clarification of the units of thought and cognition [*Denk- und Erkenntniseinheiten*] which arise from logical acts. It is preceded by an introduction in which the author attempts to give a certain account of the goals of these investigations and, in general, of the peculiarities of phenomenological clarification of knowledge in contrast to genetic-psychological clarification of it.

Theoretical thinking and cognition are accomplished in statements, i.e., in certain expressions and, closely interconnected with these, certain acts which are normally comprised under the unclear titles of "Meaning" [*Bedeutung*] or "Sense" [*Sinn*]. Naturally the epistemologically clarifying efforts are directed first of all to an analysis of the distinctions which belong to the essence of "expressing." This is the concern of the first investigation, which at every step of the way encounters deeper-seated phenomenological difficulties and, hence, on the whole has only a preparatory character.

In connection with the ideality of meanings (or rather the units of cognition associated with the meanings) discussed in this [first] investigation, the second investigation — and especially its first chapter — treats the general question of the ideality of species (of "general objects" [*allgemeine Gegenstände*, i.e., universals]) and then, in a series of chapters, critically appraises the newer theories of abstraction; the second chapter treats *Locke's* psychological

---

[1] The title of the journal was changed to include "... *und Soziologie*" in 1901 [Trans. note].

hypostatization of universals, the third chapter the attention theory of abstraction, the fourth chapter the doctrine of universal representation [*Stellvertretung*], the fifth chapter *Hume's* doctrine of the *distinctio rationis*. The final chapter gives a summary of the various concepts of abstraction and abstract.

One of these concepts of the abstract concerns abstract moments [*Momente*] — Stumpf's "partial contents" [*Teilinhalte*] or "dependent" contents. In connection with this, the third investigation discusses the general distinction between independent and dependent contents. It attempts to show that corresponding to every dependency there is a law of relation [*Zusammenhangsgesetz*] grounded in the specific nature of the content in question, in which case the distinction between these material laws and the "analytic" or categorial laws already stands out. In the further development of the ideas which are here suggested, the investigation takes the shape of an outline of a systematic theory of the doctrine of real wholes and parts according to their pure types (namely, those types which can be characterized purely categorially) and, as a result of this, an area of epistemology, somewhat neglected until now but very important, receives clarification.

‹261›   In the following investigation, the fourth, an important application of the results of the third investigation is made for clarifying the at first seemingly very trivial grammatical distinction between "categorematic" and "syncategorematic" expressions and, correspondingly, between independent and dependent meanings. The inquiry into the laws of this special class of dependencies leads to a group of laws, until now hardly touched upon, which are materially somewhat trivial but of the greatest importance for the understanding of the logical [world]. This group of laws excludes formal nonsense in contrast to purely logical laws in the usual sense which exclude formal contradiction; this group of laws prescribes which meanings can *a priori* — on the basis of their form alone — be related to another meaning regardless of whether it be a true or a false meaning, or an essentially harmonious or an essentially conflicting meaning. These "purely grammatical laws" are the ones which grant the old idea of a general and even an *a priori* grammar a safe, but admittedly very narrow sphere of legitimacy.

Next come the two main phenomenological investigations of

the volume. Their goal is the analytical elaboration of the phenomenological distinctions in which the most primitive logical distinctions find their origin. The fifth investigation goes back to the ambiguous concept of consciousness and selects three conceptions which are relevant for the clarification of knowledge: consciousness as the phenomenological unit of ego-experiences [*Icherlebnisse*], consciousness as inner perception, and consciousness as "intentional experience" [*"intentionales Erlebnis"*] or as "psychic act." This last conception of consciousness is particularly important and hence a special chapter (the second) is devoted to it. The analysis of ambiguous talk of the "content" of an act leads, among other things, to the fundamental distinction between quality and "materie" [*Materie*] (= the sense of an apprehension [*Auffassungssinn*]). The same analysis gives rise to a series of difficult deliberations which all center around the well-known statement that every psychic act is either a representation [*Vorstellung*] or has a representation as its basis. This statement proves to be unclear, even incorrect, if it is taken in the usual sense. Its lack of clarity is due to the ambiguity of the term "representation," the explication of which proves to be more important and more difficult with every step. The author offers here some fragments towards a phenomenology of representation and judgment, as a result of which one can see how much analytical work is still necessary before we can advance to a scientifically satisfactory "theory of judgment." This investigation — still in need of development and improvement on several important points — is supplemented in the final chapter by a summary of the most important equivocations of the terms "representation" and "representational content" [*Vorstellungsinhalt*].

The sixth investigation is the most extensive, most mature in content, and probably also the most fruitful one of the entire book. It is entitled: "Elements of a Phenomenological Clarification of Knowledge." Proceeding from a special problem viz., whether non-objectifying acts such as asking, wishing, ordering, and the like can also receive "expression" in the same sense as representations and judgments — the first section discusses the essence of <262> objectifying "intentions" and "fulfillments" [*Erfüllungen*] and clarifies cognition as the synthesis of objectifying fulfillment. The first chapter, "Meaning-intentions and Meaning-fulfillments," first pursues the basic relationships in the narrow sphere which was made evident in the title. The second chapter attempts to characterize indirectly the objectifying intentions and their essential modifications by means of the phenomenological distinctions of the syntheses of fulfillment. At stake are the differences between signifying (symbolic) and intuitive representations and, within the latter class, again the differences between imaginative and perceptual representations.

The third chapter outlines a phenomenology of the levels of cognition. A series of fundamental concepts are here defined. To mention only a few: the concept of the "intuitive substance" [*Gehalt*] of a representation or its "fullness" [*Fülle*]; the concepts of pure signification and pure intuition, pure imagination and pure perception; the concept of "representation" [*Repräsentation*] or apprehension [*Auffassung*]; the distinctions between the sense of apprehension, the form of apprehension and the apprehended content; the difference between complete and fragmentary intuitional experiences, between adequate and objectively complete intuitive fulfillments, etc.

The fourth chapter is a discussion of the phenomenological and ideal relationships of compatibility and incompatibility; while the fifth chapter treats the ideal of adequacy and hence the origin of the concept of self-evidence and truth (and, correspondingly being [*Sein*] in the sense of truth).

The second section of the investigation has the title: "Sensibility and Understanding." The first chapter (or rather sixth chapter in the whole series of this investigation) establishes the necessity of a fundamental — but as yet incomplete — broadening of the concepts of perception and intuitive experience [*Anschauung*][2] in such a way that these concepts embrace not only the entire sphere of external and internal sensibility (inner perception and imagination [*Einbildung*]) but also the sphere of categorial acts. There

---

[2] "*Anschauung*" has been translated as "intuitive experience" or "intuitive experiencing," and "*Intuition*," in the few places it occurs, has been rendered as "intuition." By "*Anschauung*" Husserl understands the direct observation or examination of "lived-experiences" [*Erlebnisse*] of any type whatsoever, i.e., lived-experiences of logical, mathematical and ideal entities (numbers, states of affairs, essences, etc.) and of fictional entities (literary and mythological characters) as well as physical and psychical entities (things, events, emotions, etc.). Husserl does not have any mystical or mysterious connotations in mind (cf. section 12 of the "Preface" below) [Trans. note].

is not only "perception" of "real" objects, but also of "categorial" or "ideal" objects, e.g. of ranges, of identities and non-identities, of states-of-affairs [*Sachverhalten*] of every sort, of universals, etc. In this chapter, the author believes he has revealed the foundation and cornerstone of every future phenomenology and theory of knowledge.

Passing over the next chapter which is devoted to supplementary explanations, mention must still be made of the third (or rather, the eighth) chapter which, in utilizing the preceding analyses, contrasts the apriori laws of "authentic" and "inauthentic" thinking, the former with respect to categorial intuitions and the latter with respect to categorial significations or to acts of signitively dimmed representing.

The third section has the character of an appendix. In one short chapter, it gives the clarification of the introductory problem [of this investigation].

Added to this series of investigations is a small treatise, "External and Inner Perception, Physical and Psychical Phenom- <263> ena," in which — with a critical look at Brentano's doctrine — the relationship of the distinctions indicated in the title to one another as well as to the epistemologically fundamental distinction between inadequate and adequate perception is elucidated.

It is no small venture — the author himself is well aware of this — to turn over to the public a work which is fragmentary to such an extent and still not fully clarified along several lines of thought. Originally these investigations were never intended for publication in the form in which they are here presented to the reader; they were meant only to serve the author as a basis for a more systematic grounding of epistemology or rather, of the epistemological clarification of pure logic. Unfortunately it was not possible for the author to devote another series of years to this work of many years. Nevertheless, he releases it from his hands with the conviction that, in spite of the very obvious and for him severely felt imperfections, this work because of the independence of the analytical research, because of the purity of the phenomenological method and because of a series of not unimportant new insights, will not be unwelcome to friends of epistemology. There is no lack of systematic efforts in epistemology but there is indeed a lack of fundamental analytic investigations of a strictly descriptive nature and in a spirit immune from historical prejudices.

A DRAFT OF A "PREFACE" TO THE *LOGICAL INVESTIGATIONS*

1913

I. EUGEN FINK'S EDITORIAL REMARKS

This draft of a "Preface" to the *Logical Investigations* — written in 1913, but published for the first time here — was intended by Edmund Husserl as an introduction to the revised second edition of his work. However, Husserl eventually substituted another, considerably shorter preface to the second edition in which he addresses himself primarily to the guidelines used in the revision. Only in a few places do we find anything reminiscent of the preface which is here printed for the first time.

In the short preface which accompanied the second edition printed in 1913, Husserl announced that the conclusion of the revised work would contain a critical discussion of the *typical misunderstandings* which had plagued the *Logical Investigations* time and again since their first appearance. However, this discussion did not materialize at the end of the revision completed in 1920 — it was interrupted by the World War.

However, the draft of a "Preface" published below does contain the elements of such a discussion. Therein lies its importance. It is historical evidence of a particular *self-interpretation* of Husserl's phenomenology. In coming to grips with attacks of its opponents, a philosophy characterizes itself not only by the positive exposition of its self-defense, but also by the way in which it sees its opponent and his opposition. It determines its own position in the intellectual situation of the time.

Also, in cases such as this where more than a decade of philosophical development lies between the defended work and its defense, a self-interpretation is especially revealing, since it is carried out from a higher niveau in the further development of the problems and, as such, is able to bring out *ex post* the ultimate significance of the work — i.e., its problem content, which may have remained latent originally. On the other hand, however, it is

<107> also worth noting that this interpretation of the significance of the *Logical Investigations* is not historically located in the final developmental phase of phenomenology, the phase in which Husserl had the conviction that here alone the motifs of the *Logical Investigations* achieved radical philosophical clarification and explication.

Externally considered, the development of Husserl's phenomenology falls into three phases which correspond approximately to the periods of time Husserl spent in Halle, Göttingen and Freiburg, and which are characterized by the following publications: I. *Philosophy of Arithmetic, Logical Investigations*; II. (*Lectures on*) *The Phenomenology of Internal Time Consciousness* (first published, however, in 1928), *Philosophy as a Strict Science, Ideas: A General Introduction to Pure Phenomenology*; III. *Formal and Transcendental Logic, Epilogue to My Ideas, Cartesian Meditations, The Crisis of European Sciences and Transcendental Phenomenology*.

The internal unity of the "three phases," as the history of the radicalization of a problem remains for the most part uncomprehended because the usual interpretations follow the chronology of the works instead of starting with the final form of the phenomenological program of inquiry and explicating the earlier forms which lead up to it in terms of this final form.

The place of the draft of a preface to the *Logical Investigations* here published within the total context of the evolution of phenomenology can be characterized as an *interpretation of the meaning of the first phase from the vantage of the second phase*. The fact that this draft belongs to the second phase is evident above all in the conception of phenomenology as a theory of knowledge; in the conception of the "philosophical reform of the positive sciences" as an epistemological clarification of the basic concepts of the positive sciences (through reflection upon the subject life which motivates science and yet which remains "anonymous" in the positivity of science); in the primary emphasis upon the eidetic character of the analyses of consciousness — something which comes close to being an elimination of the ontological problem as a problem of *existentia*; and finally in the polemic against the "transcendentalists" (by which is probably meant the neo-Kantian versions of transcendental philosophy).

The fact that, concerning the above mentioned points, there is a deep-reaching change in Husserl's third phase: in that the conception of philosophy has moved beyond that of a theory of knowledge; in that the idea of a philosophical reform of the sciences is radicalized to an inquiry into the foundations of the meaning of the sciences and hence moves beyond reflection upon the completed scientific meaning-constructs to the act-life [*Aktleben*] which subjectively corresponds to them; in that phenomenology comes to be seen primarily as an explication of the existing transcendental Ego, for which the analysis of essences becomes a methodological tool; in that Husserl is convinced he has fulfilled the intentions of the great transcendentalists in an analytic manner — all this is demonstrated by the works of the third phase.

Thus, in the *Formal and Transcendental Logic*, Husserl gave an interpretation of the significance of the *Logical Investigations* from the vantage of the third phase and not merely in a reconsideration of the problem in a radicalized form, but also *expressis verbis* (cf. <108> especially, Sec. 55 and thereafter).

The specific reference to the historical locus of this "Preface" which was drafted in 1913 but not published at the time is necessary therefore, because the importance of this preface today lies precisely in its value as a historical document. Its publication is not motivated by the interest in the expositions carried out in the "Preface" but solely by its value as a document of the history of phenomenology.

I would like to make one remark on terminology here: the concept of "ontology" in the following work — as is always the case with Husserl — is to be taken in a narrow sense in relation to the contemporary use of the word,[1] in as much as it does not mean a philosophical determination of being qua being [*Seienden als Seienden*] but rather an apriori eidetic of object classes [*Gegenstandsregionen*] and, more particularly, an eidetic in the naively thematic "straightforward attitude."

The division of the draft into sections and the section headings are not found in the original text; they have been added by the editor.[2]

---

[1] Fink is probably referring here to Heidegger's very different use of the term "ontology" in his works, especially *Being and Time* [Trans. note].

[2] There follows here a table of contents for the following text. It has been omitted here in light of the fact that it appears as part of the table of contents of this volume [Trans. note].

<109>

II. HUSSERL'S TEXT

Section 1. *The necessity of a preparatory introduction into the meaning of the work. — The* Logical Investigations *and the philosophical public.*

A work, such as the present one which opens up new paths for research and which, even when it revives old trends and theories, still substantially transvaluates them, should have had at its appearance a mediating introduction; a preface or an introductory chapter ought to have prepared the reader historically and topically and ought to have warned him of all of the misinterpretations which were suggested by the prevailing trends of thought. In this way the understanding of the uniqueness of the thoughts communicated and, hence, of their proper effect would surely have been promoted. I was keenly aware of this desideratum at the first edition of this work, but I was incapable of fulfilling it. There is, after all, a great difference between performing novel theoretical discoveries out of innermost necessity and in pure dedication to the demands of the subject matter on the one hand and one's being clear in reflection on the unique sense and scope of these discoveries — or rather, on the unique sense of the method employed — on the other.

There were also shortcomings in other respects. In the decade of isolated, toilsome labor in which these investigations took on an ever new and more definite form and in which no other concern mattered than to attain in pure intuition [*reiner Anschauung*] and faithful description a truly stable basis for discoveries which could seriously be called "scientific", I lost that intimate contact <110> with the contemporary literature and, hence, with the very readership to which I was to address myself.

Not even the history of philosophy could serve a mediating purpose. Much as the study of the great thinkers of the past had influenced me, I still saw all around me only undeveloped, ambiguously iridescent problems and deep-delving but unclear theories. Weary of the confusions and fearing lest I sink into the ocean of endless criticism, I felt myself compelled to push the history of philosophy aside and, for the sake of philosophical self-preservation, to risk the attempt of starting someplace on my own and to look for problems which were immediately accessible — be they ever so modest and considered of little importance — from which I could perhaps eventually work my way up step by step. At the time of the first publication of these "investigations," I had not yet come to any personal understanding with history. However, because outside circumstances would no longer allow a further delay, I allowed the "investigations" to go out into the world just as they had at that time developed, in their imperfect form that was so embarrassing even to me and in their internal unevenness and fragmentary nature. I found it very difficult to have to publish something which signified for me not an ending but rather merely an initial beginning.[1]

In view of the general character of the contemporary literature, I did not believe I could count on any serious attention. Almost without exception this literature sought its salvation partly in historical dependencies and partly in the flourishing physiological and experimental psychology. In any case, it betrayed no sensitivity for the fact that for any truly scientific philosophizing there is still need for the radical beginning sought so passionately by Descartes, for the fact that the alleged scientific grounding of epistemology through psychology is only a chain of contradictions, for the fact, on the other hand, that the great and newly developed thoughts of the Marburg School and of A. Riehl[2] concerning the Kantian critique of reason are anything but funda- ‹111› mental [grundlegende] in the true sense, i.e., derived[3] directly from the[4] most original and clearest sources (those of pure intuition), and for the fact that, as a result, the Kantian transcendental

---

[1] Compare with preface to second edition; cf. *Logical Investigations*, p. 43 [Trans. note].

[2] Alois Riehl was a German neo-Kantian philosopher who was a colleague of Husserl's on the University of Halle faculty [Trans. note].

[3] Reading "*zu schöpfende*" for "*schöpfende*" [Trans. note].

[4] Reading "*den*" for "*dem*" [Trans. note].

philosophy can neither in its original nor in its revised forms be
first philosophy in the true sense.

But contrary to all expectations, the *Logical Investigations* have
shown a rapid and to this day continuously increasing effect. It
would be difficult to show that any external factors are responsible for this. The themes treated are very dry and lie far from the
interests of any wider circle.[5] Their fundamental importance for
all approaches to the central philosophical problems could only
become comprehensible through deeper study. The attitude and
method of pure phenomenology, unfamiliar as it was, must have
had a repulsive impact even upon the professionals, who apparently intended to settle these matters in a much simpler way.
Complacent philosophers, sure of their "standpoint" could find
the phenomenological analyses and their accounts nothing other
than "speculative," "ponderous," "involved," "diffuse" and
"opaque." Nor can the attitude of the professional journals be
counted as a favorable factor behind the work's literary impact.
By far the majority of them printed no reviews whatsoever. The
only comprehensive review (dealing with both volumes) appeared
in the *Zeitschrift für Psychologie und Physiologie der Sinnesorgane*
(1903); (it is from this review that the above-quoted epithets are
taken).[6] In saying this I am ignoring the reviews of the *Literari-
sches Zentralblatt*, which said nothing and contented themselves
with a few lines. Incomplete reviews dealing with just the first
volume I found only in the *Kantstudien* (a very instructive review
by P. Natorp and, at the same time, the only one to recommend
the work — in the 1901 volume) and in the *Revue Philosophique*.
The Anglo-American journals, as far as I know, were completely
silent.

Without at this point going into a deeper consideration of the
reasons for the diverse effects of the *Logical Investigations*, I wish
to remark that these effects could in no way be entirely to my
satisfaction. Misinterpretations poured forth as much from the
side of those who praised the work as a reformatory beginning of a
‹112› methodologically original philosophy as well as from the side of

----

[5] In the German text of the *Tijdschrift* edition a printer's error destroyed the sense
of the beginning of this paragraph. The error is corrected in a footnote on the first page
of the second installment (p. 319) [Trans. note].

[6] Husserl's reply to this 1903 review has recently appeared in translation; cf. above,
p. xiii, fn. 7 [Trans. note].

those who saw in it a scholastic perversion of modern philosophy interfering with its perfectly good course of development. The misunderstandings concerned also the historical placement of the work, not to mention the usual careless construction of historical dependencies, which failed to take into account even the temporal limitations evidenced by the publication dates. Of course, the historical misinterpretations in the case of conscientiously prepared researchers also had bases in the subject matter which I myself understood only in light of the subsequent reaction.[7]

Now that I am forced finally to reissue the work, which has for a number of years been unavailable in the book trade, I can perhaps, on the basis of this understanding, be of help to the reader. Keeping in mind the motifs which determined the development of my thought, I want to try to clear up some of the most important misinterpretations and thereby to enable the reader, free from them, to take an open stance toward the actual content of the work. It is, therefore, not my intention to go into the innumerable objections for the purpose of giving a detailed rebuttal. The interested reader will easily convince himself of the fact that until now only in a few isolated instances are there any objections which are free from the sort of misinterpretations which from the very start cancel any possible relevance they might have.

Section 2. *The sense of the "Prolegomena": the separation of the logical and psychological motifs within the unity of a* SINGLE *problem; (critical discussion on Natorp[8]).*

I begin with those misunderstandings which grow out of the fact that many readers content themselves with getting to know only the "Prolegomena" or, more often, only the dispute with psychologism and think that this is enough to be able to render judgment on the sense [*Sinn*] of my epistemological-logical endeavors or on the philosophical worth of the entire work.

[7] This entire paragraph is not contained in the original 1913 draft and must have been added during one of the subsequent reworkings [Trans. note].

[8] Paul Natorp (1854–1924) was a German neo-Kantian who attempted to apply Kant's transcendental method to psychology and to the methodology of the exact sciences. Husserl held Natorp in high regard, and it was primarily Natorp who changed Husserl's negative attitude toward Kant into the very positive one which eventually resulted in Husserl's characterization of his own phenomenological philosophy as a "transcendental" idealism [Trans. note].

The reader of the "Prolegomena" is made a participant in a conflict between two motifs within the logical sphere which are contrasted in radical sharpness: the one is the psychological, the ‹113› other the purely logical. The two do not come together by accident as the thought-act on the one side and the thought-meaning [*Denkbedeutung*] and the object of thought on the other. Somehow they necessarily belong together. But they are to be distinguished, namely in this manner: everything "purely" logical is an "in itself," is an "ideal" which includes in this "in itself" — in its proper essential content [*Wesensgehalt*] — nothing "mental," nothing of acts, of subjects, or even of empirically factual persons of actual reality. There corresponds to this unique field of existing objectivities (*Objektivitäten*] a science, a "pure logic," which seeks knowledge exclusively related to these ideal objectivities, i.e., which judges on the pure meanings [*Bedeutungen*] and on the meant objectivities[9] as such (in completely pure and unqualified generality). All possible efforts are taken to dispose the reader to the recognition of this ideal sphere of being and knowledge, or, as P. Natorp expresses it, to side with "the ideal in this truly Platonic sense," "to declare oneself for idealism" with the author. Thereupon follows a task which lies in the same direction, *viz.*, to determine the natural boundary of the logical-ideal sphere (a sphere which obviously does not include all ideality whatsoever — namely, not the material *a priori* treated in the third investigation of the second volume), i.e., to grasp the idea of the pure logic in its full scope. That is the theme of the concluding chapter of the "Prolegomena": pure logic is characterized by means of a systematic development of the concept of *mathesis universalis*, which, as I tried to show, was already anticipated by Leibniz.

Nevertheless, we are by no means content with this knowledge. P. Natorp has masterfully characterized the situation in his significant review of the "Prolegomena,"[10] and though I allow myself

---

[9] "*Gegenständlichkeiten*". For Husserl, intentional acts such as cognition have an "objectifying" function, that is, these acts constitute (construct) objects in the undifferentiated flow of pure, lived-experience; they *object*ify experience. That which is constituted by such acts is something objective or object-like but not necessarily "object" in the normal sense (e.g., a tree or a house); anything can become an object of thought or reflection (e.g., "the making-of-king" or "falling in love") however, and thus a more encompassing term is needed to include anything and everything which can be objectified: an objectivity. Cf. also pp. 25–27 and 39–40 [Trans. note].

[10] *Kantstudien*, 1901, p. 282. I am quoting with a few omissions which do not

to quote the relevant passages, this is done with express mention of the fact that I am far from numbering him among the group of misinterpreting critics whom I am here really addressing. Natorp <114> says, "What remains unresolved" in these expositions of the "Prolegomena" is "the contrast between the *a priori* and the empirical, and thereby also that between the logical and the psychological, the objective and the subjective"; "the ... empirical, psychological — i.e., the real — remains left over as an uncomprehended, irrational residue which still cannot be eliminated." "And so there remains behind, even with all the, I venture to say, extraordinary lucidity of each individual logical exposition, a definite logical dissatisfaction for the reader. One follows the dramatically exciting battle of two opponents and fails to see whence ultimately their opposition stems and what it is that requires of them that they struggle for life and death — all the more since in this there becomes apparent more and more a definite interrelation and even an inseparable bond between the two, which is all the more surprising when at first one lets us see only the antagonism."

This tension, characterized so sharply in the first volume of the work, between the purely logical and the psychological and the dissatisfaction produced by it should in no way be denied. But it is not as though the author had to apologize for it. On the contrary, the discussions on psychologism would have interfered with a very essential function which they have to perform in the context of the entire work had they not aroused this dissatisfaction or had they reduced it to a lower degree by means of the presentation. Only he who feels the embarrassment of the matter deeply and in the most intense form possible, only he who sees himself compelled by the critical dissolution of the blinding prejudices of psychologism to recognize the purely logical ideal [objectivities] but who at the same time finds himself compelled by the revealing emphasis upon the essential relationships between the ideal and the psychological (as, for example, in the critique of the "theories of evidence") not to abandon by any means the psychological entirely but rather to keep it within view as somehow belonging with the ideal — only he can also have the insight that such anti-

disturb the meaning but which do qualify it in a certain way. Concerning the direction of this qualification, cf. the expositions which follow further below [Husserl's note].

psychologistic critiques are indispensable for forcing recognition of the ideal as something given prior to all theories. But also only he can have the insight that the matter can *never* end with such critiques. Only such a one can realize fully that the "being-in-
<115> itself" [*Ansichsein*] of the ideal sphere in its relation to conscious-ness brings with it a dimension of puzzles which remain untouched by all such argumentation and hence must be solved through special investigations and, in the opinion of the author, through phenomenological ones. According to the intention of the author, then, the reader would have to follow up the references to the second volume which were given in the first — i.e., he would have to look into which type of investigations are really to be deemed indispensable if the naive *mathesis universalis* (which in the natural, objective orientation and treatment is, according to the author,[11] "a matter for the mathematician") is to develop into a truly philosophical, epistemologically "clarified" pure logic. Led by the hand of the author, the reader would have to immerse him-self in the clearly limited problems of the discomforting sort which as the most accessible are to be subjected to truly adherent work for the purpose of becoming clear by means of these problems about the meaning and methodology of the accomplishments that are here wished for and eventually achieved.

Quite a few, unfortunately even the majority, of the critics of the book proceed, however, in a different manner. On the basis of a cursory glance at it, they write off the second volume. This happens, for opposite reasons, on the part of both groups: the psychologists take the investigations in question *eo ipso* as psy-chology, but as a scholastically adulterated form because there is everywhere in them talk of the ideal, of the *a priori*. But the ideal-ists (with whom I especially take issue here) find their expecta-tions of transcendental constructions from above disappointed; instead of such constructions there is everywhere talk of lived-experiences [*Erlebnissen*], acts, intentions, fulfillments, and the like — in other words, for them too, talk of the psychological. Time and again they speak of a "relapse into psychologism." They find absolutely nothing wrong with the fact that the very same author, who in the first volume displays an acuteness of judgment which they praise highly, would in the second volume seek his

[11] Cf. vol. 1, second edition, pp. 252 ff[Husserl's note].

salvation in open and outright childish contradictions. The "dis-satisfaction" which the "Prolegomena" awoke in them they charge to the author. They appease their intellectual conscience, how-ever, through quite profound but unfortunately vague and irrele- ‹116› vant generalities of the transcendental-constructionist type. I can do nothing other than consider this method of theirs every bit as "hopeless" as the psychological. Opiates suppress the symptoms; they do not cure the disease.

Section 3. *The Demand for an* INTUITIVE *method of philosophy in the return to intuitive experience* [*Anschauung*].

Problems like those having to do with the sense and object of cognition [*Erkenntnis*] are resolved neither when one subjects them to supposedly pure thought nor when one enriches the traditional philosophical vocabulary with new, profound ex-pressions but rather when one transposes these problems, which right from the outset are completely vague and ambiguous, into the light of intuitive experience by means of the laborious task of clarification, when one exemplifies them *in concreto* and finally transforms them into work problems which, at first narrow and limited, can actually be tackled within the framework of original-ly presenting, intuitive experience [*originär gebender Anschau-ung*][12] and can be led to their solution. Therefore, what is impor-tant is to look at the thinking and knowing itself, which here clearly merges with the problem, and to bring to clarity the "re-lation to objectivity" which belongs to it and which is the very thing to be grasped, as well as the sense which it finds in itself (with its relation to this objectivity); and all this is to occur ac-cording to the immanent relations which essentially belong to it and is to be considered in the light of all of the intuitively dis-tinguishable types, forms, modal modifications, intermediate stages, etc. of the new phenomena vaguely included under the title of cognition. It is for the philosophers to declare themselves radically for the principle of all principles, which demands of him

---

[12] When Husserl says that intuitive experience is "originally presenting" or "giving," he is claiming that intuitive experience is "non-theory-laden," that only the lived-experience itself [*Erlebnis*] is "presented" or "given" and that no inter-pretation or judgment is yet involved. He also calls such experience "pure" or "pre-predicative" in other places (cf. for example, *Erfahrung und Urteil*) [Trans. note].

who really strives for "absolute" cognition — and that can reason-
ably be called nothing other than radical and evident cognition in
all dimensions of possible questioning — that he precisely not
chase from above after gratuitous constructions as if one could
not get close to the affairs [*Sachen*] themselves, but rather that he
develop all knowledge from the ultimate sources — out of prin-
‹117› ciples seen directly. To this also belongs, however, that one not be
diverted by prejudices of any type, not by verbal contradictions,
not by anything in the world — even if it be called "exact science"
— and that one give that which is clearly seen its due as that
which is the "original," as that which lies prior to all theories, as
that which supplies the final criterion. The return to "the seeing"
which both ultimately clarifies and fulfills, and to the analysis
carried out in this "seeing" is admittedly no easy matter; and
every bit as difficult is the accompanying true description, as a
description given through newly developed and standardized
"concepts." Now, since it cannot be psychology which solves the
epistemological problem, then that which has to do with this too
must be fully understandable in intuition, just as it must further
be understandable from intuition what kind of a new science has
to take the place of psychology and why this new science, though
a science of "lived-experiences" [*Erlebnissen*], can nevertheless be
neither psychology nor rightfully so labeled.

This intuitive method, appealing as it does to the "affairs themselves" here under discussion, i.e., to the cognition "itself" (precisely to its direct, intuitive givenness) is what the second volume
of these *Logical Investigations* employs, which, in my opinion then,
was not written in vain even if it did not fully achieve its purposes
and in many subsidiary problems only penetrated to a partial or
one-sided intuition instead of to a full one and thus brought forth
no complete solutions at all but only the preparatory work for
them — which is, to be sure, obviously the case. Where a seemingly simple question (which then also any "philosophical novice"
could in his simplicity pose) is merely a heading for an innumerable quantity of multifaceted problems and is thus a heading for
an entire science, there the demand for a fully developed solution
and a low regard for exploratory and foundation-laying studies is
totally wrong. Whoever so proceeds with respect to philosophy
demonstrates thereby only his abandonement of the will to treat

philosophy in the sense of a genuine science or to see it so treated. Besides, the investigations of the second volume in no way remain fixed only at the level of preparatory beginnings. The method of intentional analysis of the two correlates, consciousness and ob- ‹118› jectivity,[13] is developed, and the general sense and style of the solution for the bulk of the purely logical problem, in its generality in relation to the categorial, "analytic" sphere, comes to the level of cognition in the sixth investigation. But only a few appear to have extended their readings to this last and most important investigation.

Section 4. *Repudiation of the charge of so-called "Platonism";*
ideas as objects.

Very great shock has been aroused by the "Platonism" advo-cated in the present work; I have often had to endure the charge of "Platonic hypostatization" and of the renewal of "scholastic realism." This charge is totally unjustified; it stands in sharpest contradiction to the content of my presentations and is based upon the predominance of precisely those historical prejudices from which I once with great effort had to extricate myself. The average reader is fixated right from the beginning on the view that he who teaches of ideal objects cannot avoid metaphysical hypostatization — that he can only deny it verbally. And so the average reader no longer takes the trouble to follow the sense of *my* teaching on ideal essences. My so-called "Platonism" does not consist in some sort of metaphysical or epistemological substruc-tures, hypostases [*Hypostasen*], or theories but rather in the simple reference to a type of original "givens" which usually, however, are falsely explained away. Hence I seek to convince the reader that mere prejudices are what keep him in this situation from allowing as valid that which he has indeed and without a doubt before his eyes, which he judges on countless times in everyday life and in science, which exhibits itself to him possibly in self-evident cognition and then does so as truly being — in other words, as something that is an object, that is and yet is nothing

[13] The sense of *"Gegenständlichkeit"* as "something objective or like an object" (i.e., the noematic correlate of a noetic act of "meaning" or "intending") comes out clearer here. Cf. p. 20fn. 9 above [Trans. note].

real. As an example, I refer to the ordinary predications concerning the numbers of the number series and concerning the propositions and truths of the type found in the language of pure logic
(whereby, to be sure, no judgments are made on real judgment-
acts[14]), to claims about colors, tones, conic sections, and the like
as pure types, etc. Object and predicable subject are equivalents.
<119> All logic would come to an end if the concept "object" would not
be conceived in as broad a sense as this equivalence demands —
i.e., if one did not also allow "ideas" to count as objects.

Necessarily connected with the comprehension and categorial
judgment of ideas as objects stand the possibilities for "un-
conditional" universal judgments about "objects in general" as
conceived through ideas specified by predicates, i.e., the possibilities for judgments of pure ideal universality. All such judgments
imply not the slightest claim about anything real; their meaning
and validity is independent of whether or not there is even a
reality of any kind. Even whether or not a reality is possible
cannot be inferred from such judgments — unless the idea of
reality or its derivative ideas enter into such judgments from the
outset, namely, if they are themselves ideal judgments [*Ideal-
urteile*] about the (thinkable, possible in ideal terms) real. These
are indicators — not theories. What they reveal precedes all
theory and basically also all "theory of knowledge." In a naive
sense, then, everyone is a "Platonist," namely, everyone who
makes "ideal-science-type" [*idealwissenschaftliche*] judgments
without worrying about philosophical justifications, just as everyone in a naive sense is an "empiricist" who makes "natural-
science-type" [*realwissenschaftliche*] judgments, such as judgments
about plants, tables, etc. in a similarly nonchalant way. The
reference to what is intended in this naïveté and is possibly given
as existent (a reference which yields upon simple observation two
"original" and "originally" distinguishable types of objectivities
— original because it is comprehensible in immediate "observation") precedes, I repeat, all theories and also all philosophies. Of
course, the deepest philosophical problems are attached to the

---

[14] Husserl apparently means here that, in the language of pure logic, no judgments
are made concerning the status — real, ideal, etc. — of the logical acts (of making
judgments) themselves. Only the logical judgment-acts qua judgment-acts are in
question in pure logic, not the metaphysical or ontological nature of such acts [Trans.
note].

givenness [*Gegebenheit*] and to the "being" to be given [*zu gebendes
"Sein"*], and, of course, these problems differentiate themselves
according to the basic types of givenness and their correlative[15]
basic types of objects. But what precedes this problematic and
what specifies its sense is that one just looks at the types of being
and givenness, accepts them from the beginning simply as ob-
servables, and brings to mind the realization that no theory can ‹120›
eliminate what is the ultimate standard for all theory: that which
is given in plain seeing and is, therefore, original. If someone
wanted to prove to us through ever so impressive philosophical
arguments that, because of a psychologically explainable illusion,
all of our empirical judgments about things are only apparently
about things, that only what is immanent within consciousness
can really be perceived, conceived, or judged (to wit, sense-data,
act qualities, and the like) — we would immediately reflect and
answer: I am presently making a judgment about the table over
there. That is obviously no sensation-experience [*Empfindungs-
erlebnis*], no act quality, or anything of the sort. It is, as opposed
to all "immanent" data something "transcendent." The judgment may be false, but the fact that what is here "perceived" and
"judged" is precisely a table (something transcendent) is absolutely certain. I can simply look at that which is *meant as such* and
can grasp it absolutely. There is no evidence that could ever be
superior to this. One cannot philosophize away anything thus
seen; it is in all proper philosophizing the ultimate standard. It
is exactly the same when it comes to the ideal. If, for example, the
Marty school assures us that judgments such as those about the
number series are only apparently about ideal objects termed *the*
two, *the* three, etc., and that in truth one is here making judgments about real things, and if they assure us that all talk of ideal
objects, as for example, of propositions, are for such and such
reasons a "fiction," then I reply again: No evidence is ever capable
of overruling that which I, in judging now about *the* two, three,
etc. or about the pure meaning of, say, a geometrical proposition,
possess in absolute direct grasp of what is therein intended as such
and, in the case of insight, of that which is therein given. And just
as absolute is the evidence that such a pure judgment asserts

---

[15] Reading "*korrelativen*" for "*Korrelativen*" [Trans. note].

nothing about reality and that any dragging in of the real distorts its sense, not even maintaining the rule of equivalence.

Section 5. *The concept of pure logic as* MATHESIS UNIVERSALIS *(the unity of the "analytic" doctrine of forms for that which can be an object on the one hand with the categories of meaning on the other). The "positivity" of logic and the* <121> *philosophical problem of its phenomenological elucidation. — Positive science in general and phenomenology.*

I turn now to the misinterpretations having to do with my idea of a "pure logic" which present themselves in various ways depending on the standpoint from which the philosophical reader approaches the *Logical Investigations*. It might be best here if I meet these misinterpretations by pointing out positively what is essential to my position with special emphasis upon the points which have not received enough attention.

"Pure logic," in its most comprehensive[16] extension characterizes itself by an essential distinction as *"mathesis universalis."* It develops through a step-by-step extension of that particular concept of formal logic which remains as a residue of pure ideal doctrines dealing with "propositions" and validity after the removal from traditional logic of all the psychological misinterpretations and the normative-practical goal positings [*Zielgebungen*]. In its thoroughly proper extension it includes all of the pure "analytical" doctrines of mathematics (arithmetic, number theory, algebra, etc.) and the entire area of formal theories, or rather, speaking in correlative terms, the theory of manifolds [*Mannigfaltigkeitslehre*] in the broadest sense. The newest development of mathematics brings with it that ever new groups of formal-ontological laws are constantly being formulated and mathematically treated which earlier had remained unnoticed. *"Mathesis universalis"* as an idea includes the sum total of this formal *a priori*. It is, in the sense of the "Prolegomena," directed toward the entirety of the "categories of meaning" [*Bedeutungskategorien*] and toward the formal categories for objects correlated to them or, alternatively, the *a priori* laws based upon them. It thus includes the entire *a priori* of what is in the most fundamental

---

[16] Reading *"umfassendsten"* for *"unfassendsten"* [Trans. note].

sense the "analytic" or "formal" sphere — a sense which receives a strict specification and clarification in the third and sixth investigations. I would like to mention, incidentally, that the propriety of this delimitation can be made evident first in the naive-natural perspective and that it must retain its value in any case also for those who reject my "idealism" on psychologistic grounds. Thus no psychologistic empiricism *à la* Mill can change the fact ‹122› that pure mathematics is a strictly self-contained system of doctrines which is to be cultivated using methods that are essentially different from those of natural science. He has to recognize the present distinction even if he wants to reinterpret it later on. And, conversely, even an adherent of psychologism [*Psychologist*][17] could, if there were as yet no geometry, understand and approve the demonstration of the necessity of such a discipline in its fundamental peculiarity as opposed to natural science — he would just interpret it subsequently in his own style.

The *mathesis universalis* in its so-to-say naive as well as in its technical forms, as it has been grounded in the natural-objective orientation and can then be further cultivated, has at first no common cause with epistemology and phenomenology — just as little as ordinary arithmetic (a subdivision of *mathesis universalis*) has. However, if it also assumes the problem of the phenomenological "elucidation" in the sense of the "Prolegomena" and of the second volume, if as a consequence of this it learns from the sources of phenomenology what the solution is to the great riddles which here as everywhere arise from the correlation between being and consciousness, if in the process it learns as well the ultimate formulation of the meaning of concepts and[18] propositions (a formulation which only phenomenology is capable of providing): then it will have transformed itself from the naive into the truly philosophical pure logic, and it is in this sense that the pure logic is spoken of in philosophical contexts as a philosophical discipline. Examined precisely (and in harmony with the most recent accounts in my *Ideas*), it is not a mere coupling of phenomenology of knowledge with natural-objective *mathesis* but is rather an

[17] The English term "psychologist" is rendered as "*Psychologe*" in German; the German term "*Psychologist*" designates one who is an adherent of the logical or epistemological position of psychologism, while "*Psychologe*" designates simply one trained in the science of psychology. [Trans. note].

[18] Reading "*und*" for "*une*" [Trans. note].

application of the former to the latter.[19] In a similar manner the physical theory of nature, for example, changes from mere natural science in the traditional sense of "positive" science into philosophy of nature by introducing the epistemological problematic belonging to it and its step-by-step solution through phenomenology. This describes, however, nothing other than a physics which has been both philosophically deepened and enriched by all of the <123> problems concerning the correlation of physical being and cognitive subjectivity, a physics in which the experiencing subjectivity that performs the methodological achievement of objective knowledge does not remain scientifically anonymous and in which the methodical as well as the pertinent basic concepts and basic propositions are developed from the very beginning in ultimate methodological originality. Philosophical physics does not begin, as does the naive-positive physics, with vague concepts and then proceed in naively practiced methodical technique. It is from the very beginning a science that comprehends itself radically and that justifies right up to the end its constitution of sense and being [*Sinn- und Seinskonstitution*]. So the task is everywhere the same: to transform the merely positive sciences into "philosophical" ones or, where new sciences have to be established, to establish them from the very outset as "philosophical." Above all, philosophy means not irrelevant, speculative mysticism but rather nothing other than the ultimate radicalization of *rigorous* science. To be sure, positive science itself is trying to realize this ideal, but in its abstract one-sidedness, which is blind to the correlation in cognition, it is incapable of satisfying this ideal.[20]

At the same time, one can now understand my paralleling the idea of a "pure" — or better, "formal" — logic with the regional[21] ontologies parallel to it. Just as formal logic refers to the formal

---

[19] The German text in *Tijdschrift* reads: "*eine Umwendung der ersteren in die letztere*" ("a transformation of the former into the latter") which is clearly a transcription or printing error that says the opposite of what Husserl means. Husserl's 1913 shorthandmanuscript — upon which our translation of this sentence is based — reads: "*eine Anwendung der ersteren an die letzteren.*" Thus, natural-objective *mathesis* is transformed into philosophical *mathesis* through the application of phenomenology [Trans. note].

[20] These last sentences express the basic theme which Husserl developed in his 1911 *Logos* article "Philosophy as Rigorous Science" [Trans. note].

[21] Reading "*regionalen*" for "*rationalen.*" "*Rational* ontologies" does not make sense in this context and is obviously a transcription or printing error. Two lines later, the German reads "*regionalen*" with respect to the same idea [Trans. note].

idea of object, to the "something in general." and can be characterized as formal ontology, so the regional ontologies refer to the highest material classes of objects whatsoever which (in the *Ideas*) are designated as "regions." If one chooses to call even these *a priori*, regional disciplines "logics," then, for example, Kant's pure science of nature, expanded to a universal ontology of nature in general, would have to be characterized as a logic of nature. Geometry, as a self-contained ontological discipline, would fit into it as the logic of pure (idealized) spatiality. Then, there corresponds again to every such "naive" logic to be constructed in the "natural-objective" orientation a "philosophical" logic that is an epistemologically and phenomenologically clarified one or one that is phenomenologically grounded from the very beginning. Whereas for pure logic in the sense of the present work (an "ana- <124> lytics" understood in the broadest and radical sense) only certain of the most general cognitive-formations [*Erkenntnisgestaltungen*] enter the picture for purposes of phenomenological elucidation, by contrast, for the material ontologies, in addition to the general cognitive-formations, also the corresponding cognitive-formations specifically related to the subject matter are to be drawn into the elucidating consideration of essences. Thus, for the ontology or logic of a possible (merely physical) nature in general, the basic forms of the subjective modes of knowledge used in constituting nature are introduced, and for the ontology of the soul or the mind, the forms related to its constitution are included. This takes care of an acute objection of P. Natorp (*loc. cit.*) that rested on a misunderstanding which did have a basis insofar as the text of my writing lacked an exposition of the sort just given, although this does not mean that for the single purpose I had focused upon — *viz.*, a philosophical elucidation of the sphere of "pure logic" — there was any real shortcoming.[22]

---

[22] The longhand section of the 1913 manuscript of this draft ends here; the shorthand portion begins with the next section (Sec. 6) which Husserl had originally numbered Section 1 — cf. translators' introduction, text-critical notes [Trans. note].

Section 6. *The* Logical Investigations *as a breakthrough work.* —
*The antecedent history of its problematic: the beginning
with the questions about the psychological origin of basic
mathematical concepts; the study of Lotze and Bolzano.*
— *The thematic orientation of the mathematician; its
naive justification and the problem of a phenomenological
turn.*

Above all it must be said that in the conviction of the author
— already just hinted at — a breakthrough really did take place
with this work: the breakthrough of an essentially new science
— pure phenomenology — and the breakthrough of a newly
grounded philosophy; grounded, actually, as phenomenology.[23]
It is understandable that it happens here just as with an initial
breakthrough of any kind: the old mixes in here and there with
the new, and the author, even with all the vivid awareness of this
newness (an awareness that can be seen in the work itself), was
at the time of the first edition not yet in full command of it and in
many respects had also not achieved final clarity. In my own
<125> announcement of the second volume in the *Vierteljahrsschrift für
wissenschaftliche Philosophie*, 1901, I gave public expression to
this state of affairs. It closes with the words,

> It is no small venture — the author himself is well aware of this —
> to turn over to the public a work which is fragmentary to such an
> extent and still not fully clarified along several lines of thought.
> Originally these investigations were never intended for publication in
> the form in which they are here presented to the reader; they were
> meant only to serve the author as a basis for a more systematic
> grounding of epistemology or rather, of the epistemological clarifi-
> cation of pure logic. Unfortunately it was not possible for the author
> to devote another series of years to this work of many years. Neverthe-
> less, he releases it from his hands with the conviction that, in spite of
> the very obvious and for him severely felt imperfections, this work,
> because of the independence of the analytical research, because of the
> purity of the phenomenological method and because of a series of not
> unimportant new insights, will not be unwelcome to friends of episte-
> mology. There is no lack of systematic efforts in epistemology but
> there is indeed a lack of fundamental analytic investigations of a
> strictly descriptive nature and in a spirit immune to historical pre-
> judices.

[23] The German text in *Tijdschrift* reads "*gegründet als Phänomenologie*" and we
have translated this; the original 1913 manuscript, however, reads "*gegründet durch
Phänomenologie*" ("grounded by phenomenology") and this would seem to make

In view of this state of affairs, therefore, the author himself occasionally fell into misconstruing interpretations of the sense of his intentions and of the techniques of investigation which, in the framework of the selected problems, were approached essentially in the right manner. The younger generation finds something like this hard to understand. But there are errors into which the author himself lapses much easier than the youth which follow him. Manners of thinking whose irrationality he has exposed no longer become for the youth habits of thought, but they are, by contrast, still operative in the author as dispositions — dispositions to relapses — acquired through education. The important point to which this remark is directed with special force will be more precisely articulated later.

The breakthrough of phenomenology is tied to investigations which already occupied the author for years previously, investigations first of all for the purpose of elucidating the cognitive ‹126› accomplishment of arithmetic and of pure analytical mathematics in general. Above all it was its purely symbolic procedural techniques, in which the genuine, originally insightful sense seemed to be interrupted and made absurd under the label of the transition through the "imaginary" [entities], that directed my thoughts to the signitive [*das Signative*] and to the purely linguistic aspects of the thinking — and knowing — process and from that point on forced me to carry out general "investigations," which concerned universal ·clarification of the sense, the proper delimitation, and the unique accomplishment of formal logic. In view of my entire training, it was obvious to me when I started that what mattered most for a philosophy of mathematics was a radical analysis of the "psychological origin" of the basic mathematical concepts. In my habilitation thesis of 1887 (from which a piece has been printed as an academic dissertation and which in 1891 — but in a somewhat more expanded presentation of the original thought-content — appeared under the title, *Philosophie der Arithmetik*; *Psychologische und logische Analysen*, *I*),24 I dealt with the "origin" of the concepts of plurality, number, unity, and the associated

better sense in that Husserl usually speaks of phenomenology as the method which grounds a phenomenological, transcendental philosophy [Trans. note].

24 Lothar Eley has recently brought out a critical edition of this early work along with numerous appendices containing related material; cf. *Husserliana XII* (Den Haag: Martinus Nijhoff, 1970) [Trans. note].

primitive operational concepts for addition, etc. Here for the first time I hit upon a basic form of the synthetically multi-directional consciousness which takes its place among the basic forms of "categorial" consciousness in the sense of the *Logical Investigations*. And with the question about the relationship of the collective forms in contrast to these unitary forms, I hit upon the distinction between sensuous and categorial unity; in the terminology taken over from Mill, I called every whole, every combination a "relation," and thus the difference appears terminologically as the distinction between the psychical and content relations. The further question about the origin of the idea of symbolic sets [*uneigentlichen Mengenvorstellungen*] led to the "quasi-qualitative or figureal" moments [*Momente*] which are made up out of the "fusions" of such content relations — the same moments which had been termed gestalt-qualities by Ehrenfels[25] in his well-known monograph which appeared in 1890 (but which was prompted by entirely different problems).

<127>   Much as I saw in my analyses helpful and new beginnings, they still left me deeply dissatisfied. I had already hit upon the distinction between what an idea [*Vorstellung*] "means" and what is contained in it, and yet I did not know what to do about it. The idea of "set" [*Menge*] was supposed to arise out of the collective combination (out of unifying consciousness of meaning-together [*Zusammenmeinens*], in the conceiving-as-one [*Ineinsbegreifens*]) and certainly, there was some truth in that. The collective is no substantial unity grounded in the content of the collected items; in accordance with the school model which I had been taught which holds that everything that can be grasped intuitively had to be either "physical" or "psychical," it could not be physical: hence, the concept of collection arises through psychological reflection in Brentano's[26] sense, i.e., through "reflection" upon the

[25] Christian von Ehrenfels (1859–1932) was a German philosopher who, like Husserl, had studied under Franz Brentano in Vienna. He is best known for his work in Gestalt psychology and value theory. [Trans. note].

[26] Franz Brentano (1838–1917) was a German philosopher who attempted to combine Aristotelianism, neo-scholasticism and empiricism in his philosophy. He exercised a profound influence on so many German philosophers of his day that a "Brentano school" eventually grew up. As Husserl's primary mentor in philosophy, Brentano is almost completely responsible for the direction of Husserl's thought in his early years; and, as the discoverer of the notion of "intentionality" in the sense of "referring to an object," Brentano is also very much responsible for Husserl's discovery of phenomenology [Trans. note].

act of collecting just as the concept of unity arises from reflection
upon the act of positing-as-something. But then is the concept of
number not something basically different from the concept of
collecting which is all that can result from the reflection on acts?
Such doubts unsettled — even tormented — me already in the
very beginnings and then extended to all categorial concepts as I
later called them and finally in another form to all concepts of
objectivities of any sort whatsoever. The customary appeal in the
Brentano school to symbolic representation[27] — representation
via relations — could not help. That was only a phrase in the place
of a solution.

These ambiguities found ever new nourishment in the contexts
of the expanded philosophical-arithmetic studies, which extended
to the broadest field of modern analysis and theory of manifolds
and simultaneously to mathematical logic and to the entire sphere
of logic in general.[28] The immense importance that "purely
symbolic thinking" has for consciousness could, after all sorts of
difficulties, theoretically be comprehended by external logic, as it
were, in the case of mathematics. But how symbolic thinking is
"possible," how the objective, mathematical, and logical relations ‹128›
constitute themselves in subjectivity, how the insight into this is
to be understood, and how the mathematical in itself, as given in
the medium of the psychical, could be valid, this all remained a
mystery.

The fruit of these studies was, on the one side, the so-to-say
ontological demarcation of the pure *mathesis universalis*, an idea
which I rediscovered in my historical studies on Leibniz and, on
the other side, the dissociation in principle from psychologism —
in other words, the first part of the present work. For, although
this part received its literary format only at a later time, its content is in its essentials, and especially in all of its anti-psycholo-
gistic argumentation, only a reproduction of my university
lectures from the summer and autumn of 1895 — which also

[27] "*Uneigentliches Vorstellen*" has been translated as "symbolic representation" in
spite of the fact that "uneigentlich" literally means "inauthentic." We have done so
on the basis that Husserl states in the *Philosophie der Arithmetik* that "uneigentlich"
means the same thing as "symbolic" in relation to thinking and representation; cf.
Husserliana XII, pp. 181–256, esp. p. 193ff. [Trans. note].

[28] Of the investigations relative to this, only two small treatises reached (in autumn
of 1893) literary completion and were published in 1894 (*Philosophische Monatshefte*,
vol. XXIX) [Husserl's note].

accounts for a certain liveliness and freedom in the presentation. The only section that was really freshly composed was the concluding chapter, whose thought-content, however, stems entirely from the older logical-mathematical studies, on which I had not worked any further since 1894.

As the reader can see, the studies of the author in these years of 1886–1895 confined themselves primarily to the, to be sure, very comprehensive but still limited areas of formal mathematics and formal logic. The dissociation from psychologism takes place first of all on the basis of studies in this area, although at the same time it occurs in the most general attention to the entire sphere even though it has not yet been taken up, to any appreciable degree, in actual research. This transformation was prepared by the study of Leibniz and by the considerations occupying me ever anew of the sense both of the distinction between truths of reason and truths of fact and also at the same time of Hume's expositions concerning knowledge about "relations of ideas" and "matter [sic] of fact." I became keenly aware of the contrast between this latter distinction and Kant's distinction between analytic and synthetic judgments, and this became important for the later positions which I took.

For the fully conscious and radical turn and for the accompanying "Platonism," I must credit the study of Lotze's[29] logic. Little as Lotze himself had gone beyond [pointing out] absurd inconsistencies and beyond psychologism, still his brilliant interpretation of Plato's doctrine of Ideas gave me my first big insight and was a determining factor in all further studies. Lotze spoke already of truths in themselves, and so the idea suggested itself to transfer all of the mathematical and a major part of the traditionally logical [world] into the realm of the ideal. With regard to the logic which before I had interpreted psychologistically and which had perplexed me as a mathematical logician,[30] I, thanks to a fortunate circumstance, no longer needed extensive and detailed deliberations as to its separation from the psychological [sphere].

<129>

[29] R. H. Lotze (1817–1881) was a German philosopher and scientist who attempted to combine scientific empiricism, philosophical idealism and religious theism by distinguishing three separate spheres — necessary truths, facts and values — within one absolute substance, God [Trans. note].

[30] The original 1913 manuscript reads: "which as mathematical logic had perplexed me" [Trans. note].

Bolzano[31] as a mathematician was brought to my attention (I was a student of Weierstrass[32] at the time) through an article by Stolz in the *Mathematische Annalen,* and above all through Brentano's critical discussion (in his lectures) of the "paradoxes of infinity," and through G. Cantor.[33] After that I made a point of looking through the long-forgotten *Wissenschaftslehre [Theory of Science]* of 1837 and of making use of it from time to time with the help of its copious index. However, his original thoughts about ideas, propositions and truths "in themselves," I misinterpreted as metaphysical abstrusities.[34]

Then it suddenly occurred to me (at first with respect to the traditional sphere of logic) that the first two volumes of Bolzano's *Wissenschaftslehre* (entitled "A Theory of Ideas in Themselves" and "A Theory of Propositions in Themselves") were to be looked upon as a first attempt at a unified presentation of the area of pure ideal doctrines — in other words, that here a complete plan of a "pure" logic was already available. Understandably, this insight offered me an immense benefit: step by step using Bolzano's account, I could verify the "Platonic" interpretation which was ⟨130⟩ admittedly far from Bolzano's intentions.[35] But as I thereupon

[31] B. Bolzano (1781–1848) was an Austrian philosopher and mathematician whose work in logic anticipated many aspects of contemporary symbolic logic and mathematics [Trans. note].

[32] Karl Weierstrass (1815–1897) was a brilliant German mathematician who is best known for his work in the formal arithmetization of mathematics. Husserl studied under Weierstrass in Berlin during the years 1878–1881 and was his assistant during the year 1883/84 [Trans. note].

[33] Georg Cantor (1845–1918) was a German mathematician who is best known as the founder of the theory of transfinite cardinal and ordinal numbers. He was professor of mathematics at the University of Halle (1872–1913) during the same years Husserl was studying and teaching philosophy there (1886–1901), and exercised considerable influence upon Husserl's work in philosophy of mathematics, especially his attempts to axiomatize set theory (cf. *Husserliana XII,* p. xxiii) [Trans. note].

[34] Rickert's[36] opinion that Bolzano had been a well-known, much-used, and influential scholar in Austria is a fabrication without the slightest factual basis — just as is the majority of what he says about Brentano, about me, and about our relations to Bolzano. As for how things stood with regard to Bolzano's impact may be seen already from the fact that even around 1901 the original edition (1837) of the *Wissenschaftslehre* was still not sold out and that, finally, the Braumüller partial edition of 1884 was thrown onto the market in second-hand stores at give-away prices — very shortly before my new discovery of his importance began turning the general attention towards him [Husserl's note].

[35] The practice (which now seems to be so popular) of projecting my own views back upon Bolzano (obviously without taking the trouble of a real study of the *Wissenschaftslehre*) produces a picture of Bolzano that is totally distorted historically [Husserl's note].

[36] Heinrich Rickert (1863–1936) was a German philosopher who attempted to work out a transcendental idealistic system of philosophy much along the same lines as the

set to work (on the basis of the new insight and with the aid of Bolzano) at completely revising my lectures on logic, I recognized the incompleteness of Bolzano's plan. It lacked the idea of a purely formal mathematics or, correspondingly, a "universal theory of manifolds," which I had worked out in such purity through my systematic and historical studies (as was at that time by no means in any way familiar to mathematicians as it is, however, today). And in line with this it lacked also any awareness of the inner unity of formal logic with pure theory of numbers, theory of magnitudes, etc. and ultimately with pure theory of manifolds and theory of theories. In connection with this there was not even a beginning of a discussion on the relation between formal onto-logical and formal semantical considerations, which in its own right is connected with the lack of any clarification of the concepts "proposition in itself" and "idea in itself." There was missing both the contrast between proposition (as logical judgment) and state of affairs as well as all of other fundamental distinctions which pertain thereto.

I reflected a great deal upon the relationship between formal-*ontological* propositions to which I, by starting out from mathematical studies, was at first compelled to give preference (i.e., propositions concerning objects as such, states of affairs, pluralities, series, etc. as such), and, on the other hand, propositions about *meanings* (about propositions and possible proposition-components as such). The full result of these studies did not, to be sure, reach publication in the *Logical Investigations* (it is tucked away for the most part in my unpublished lectures on logic), but out of them did arise both the fundamental distinction of logical categories into categories of meaning and formal, object-related <131> (formal-ontological) categories as well as the relationship of logic as *mathesis universalis* to all *a priori* truths, which are grounded in the two types of categories. And the same holds for the short presentation of the general guidelines for the demarcation of a subdivision of logic on the side of a formal theory of meaning (namely, a pure, or, better yet, a purely logical grammar as a special *a priori* discipline), i.e. the presentation of the fourth

German idealist Johann Fichte (1762–1814) had. Husserl corresponded with Rickert and assumed Rickert's chair of philosophy in Freiburg in 1916 when he retired [Trans. note].

investigation of the second volume and, to no less an extent, the third (which provides a portion of the *a priori* theory of wholes and parts, i.e. of the forms of combinations and of unity).

In all these "pure-logical" studies there was no mention of epistemology. No epistemology lies in "Platonism," but, on the contrary, the simple inner acceptance of something that is manifestly given — of something that lies prior to all theory and also to all "theory of knowledge." If, following the evidence of experience and ultimately of originally giving perception in its harmonious progression, we speak straightforwardly about things that are, if we pass normal judgments about them, if we cultivate science, we simply accept what is immediately given to us as that which is, and we inquire into its properties and laws. If we likewise, untroubled over all controversy, for example, between Platonism and Aristotelianism, speak of numbers of "the" number series, of propositions, of pure classes and types of formal as well as material givens (as, for example, the mathematician as arithmetician or geometrician does), we are not yet epistemologists. We follow the evidence which such "ideas" *give* us, and it is still a long way from any epistemology if we merely say in the face of such conflicts: These sorts of objectivities [*Gegenständlichkeiten*], though not "given through the senses" and not perceived objectivities in the usual sense, are still given evidentially, and they are evidently substrata of valid predications. They are therefore objectivities and, to distinguish them from empirical objectivities, we call them "ideal objectivities." But all the same it is a primary and entirely necessary step for the posing of intelligent epistemological questions to talk in this way and not to allow oneself right away to be talked out of ideas as givens. But all inclinations to distorting interpretations stem from the basic diffi- ‹132› culties in the understanding of being and consciousness — both taken in a very broadened sense. And in this connection arises the necessity of adding to the so-called naive *mathesis universalis* (or "pure logic") — which is framed or to be framed unconcerned about any theory of knowledge — a philosophy of this *mathesis* which would be a "theory of mathematical knowledge," a certain elucidation of its possible true meaning and of its right to validity. The investigations concerning this field (and the broader field of the not only formal but also material regions of knowledge), which in awkward beginnings had already preceded long ago, filled the years up to the last finished version of the *Logical Investigations* — i.e., up to 1899.[37] In these years of concentrated work (sometimes hopeful but much more often despairing) developed the specifically phenomenological investigations (the first, second, fifth, and sixth investigations and the phenomenological ingredients in the remainder of the second volume).

Only the thoughts of a much later period made it clear to me that if the naivete of every positive science (including the *mathesis universalis* in the naive treatment as a positivity directed straight toward the envisioned ideal) required an epistemological "clarification" — i.e., required a deeper grounding of the justification [*Rechtes*] and limits of its authenticity of sense [*Sinnesechtheit*] and required the systematic study of subjective and intersubjective modes of cognition that are essentially inseparable from objective ideals — then no positive science of any sort can justify itself. These later thoughts also made it clear to me that only a science that is grounded from the very beginning upon "transcendental phenomenology" and that flows from it to the principal original sources can correspond to the full idea of an absolutely justified knowledge.[38] The stage we call positive science may be an historical fact, but this stage must be surmounted in a universal reform of science which cancels [*aufhebt*] any distinction between positive science and a philosophy to be opposed to it or which transforms all sciences at once into philosophical sciences and gives pure phenomenology the value of a universal fundamental-science — of a first philosophy.

<133>　　This account can thus serve to dispel a number of important misunderstandings related to the idea of pure logic as well as some concerning the relationship between these *Logical Investigations* and the theories of Lotze and Brentano.[39]

---

[37] This date — 1899 — which Husserl gives for the final finished version of the *Logical Investigations* is dubious. In a letter to his good friend Gustav Albrecht in 1901, Husserl says that he was still working on the analyses of the sixth investigation during the winter 1900/01 [Trans. note].

[38] A printing error which destroyed the sense of this sentence and the next is corrected in the footnote to page one of the second installment (*Tijdschrift*, p. 319) [Trans. note].

[39] The German text in *Tijdschrift* reads "Brentano" but this is obviously a transcription error, for Husserl has only discussed Lotze and *Bolzano* in this section. The original 1913 shorthand manuscript simply has "B." which usually stood for "Bren-

Section 7. *Critical discussion of Meinong.* — *Demarcations in the* <319>
*region of the a priori: The distinction between 1) the
formal and material a priori, and 2) the "phenomenological" and "ontological" a priori.*

Some of the confusion in the interpretation of the pure logic has
been engendered by its relation to the alleged "discovery" of a
"theory of objects."

The idea of an *a priori* or rational ontology is actually an age-
old matter. Everyone knows how many sorts of ontological
sciences with contents of, at least, pretended *a priori* cognition
have been tried in the course of time. Because of a very understandable tendency to identify being with real being, ontology
meant the *a priori* science of real being. Furthermore, because the
idea of a formal and material *a priori* of being in general was never
clearly distinguished, it was legitimate to consider the various <320>
ontological sciences also as *one* science — similar to the way that
the various disciplines of natural science ("empirical ontologies"
or "empirical theories of being" as it were) are considered branches
of the one science of nature. All realities do go together within
empirical reality — but, as is to be expected, also in the idea — to
[become] the unity of a world. To begin with, the attack of Kant-
ianism against the inauthentic and metaphysical (in the bad sense)
ontologies of its day (in and alongside which admittedly the beginnings also of a good ontology are demonstrable) and, even more,
the successful advance of empirical philosophy in the second half
of the last century have deprived ontology of its creditability.
Only empirical natural science was allowed and, along with it, a
mathematics that was empirically reinterpreted — even though
it remained, despite this reinterpretation, isolated in radical
methodical diversity. In addition to all of this, there was at best a
medium of vague epistemology. But in my investigations the idea
of ontology in a peculiar form was revived without any historical
allusions and hereby also free from radical obscurities and errors
which adhered to the old ontologies and which justified the opposition to them.

If one takes what is present in the work here published and if

tano" in Husserl's shorthand and was thus probably so transcribed by Stein or Landgrebe, but Husserl clearly means "Bolzano" here and not "Brentano" [Trans. note].

one understands under ontology in its proper generality any purely rational science of objects — any science constructing itself from pure essential insights, any science constituting itself in the intuition of essences and free from all positings of individual being — then the *mathesis universalis* is demonstrated to be an ontology. (Only the word is avoided in the first edition.) It is expressly characterized as the *a priori science of objects in general* and, correlatively, of meanings in general, which refer to objects in general. That is already expressed as sharply as it ever could be in the first volume and then again anew in the second. And so no one who had really read the work had the slightest reason to instruct me about the "object-theoretical" [*"gegenstandstheoretischen"*] character of formal logic and mathematics. In addition, the entire ‹321› third investigation of the second volume announces[40] itself expressly as belonging to the *"a priori* theory of objects as such,"* and it is, in any case, this passage which has led to the little-to-be-recommended coining of the expression, "theory of objects."

Newly opened up on this occasion was the self-contained *a priori* discipline of *pure logical grammar* as an *a priori* study of those forms of meanings which I obviously include in the idea of a *mathesis* (just as I do the study of the validity of meanings) since it just will not work to assign to different disciplines cognitions that belong together as correlates and that are *equivalent* to so great an extent. But ontology or theory of objects taken in the broadest sense mentioned above is not only all that which relates to the field of pure *mathesis* (that would include the entire first volume and the third and fourth investigations of the second) but also the entire first volume of the work [can be considered as ontology or theory of objects] insofar as the whole approach whereby the overcoming of psychologism is phenomenologically accomplished shows that what the author had given as analyses of immanent consciousness must be considered as a pure *a priori* analysis of essence. In this way were opened up for the first time, and in far-reaching analyses actually carried out, the immense fields of the givens of consciousness as fields for "ontological" investigations. The starting point for all this lay in intensive studies of Hume's relations among ideas compared to Leibniz' truths of reason, to Kant's analytic truths, and, at the same time,

---

[40] Reading *"kündigt"* for *"kündet"* [Trans. note].

to the Lotze studies, of which I have already spoken. Lotze had regarded the realm of sense-data, of color- and sound-data, as a field of ideal, and thus "ontological", cognitions. What he did not see was that consciousness itself, the immense wealth of intentional experiences and noematic correlates in experience, was an infinitely richer field of *a priori* knowledge and something that is fully accessible to systematic research, that its systematically coherent, pure exploration is precisely the vital question for an "exact" psychology and a serious epistemology. The resumption of Platonic thoughts and, simultaneously, the interpretation of the "insight" in which relations among ideas are given to us as a <322> "seeing," as an *originally presenting consciousness*, necessitated already at an early point that I ascribe an *essence* to *all* objectivities and hence a field of essence-cognitions — if one will, of theory of object-like cognitions. Because of the convictions which dominate the present work, this was completely obvious. But it never occurred to me simply to adopt under the title of ontology or theory of objects a science as a correlate to the reservoir of all *a priori* cognitions and sciences. It is not the task of the philosopher to throw together but rather to search for and to fix the demarcations between essences. And so throughout many years my efforts were directed towards working out the proper concept of the analytical as opposed to the unclear Kantian one and towards finding what is indeed for philosophy the *fundamental distinction* which separates the proper analytic ontology from the material (synthetic-*a priori*) ontology, which is to be separated from it fundamentally. Only after the publication of the *Logical Investigations* did I set for myself the task of distributing all the demarcations within being. I told myself that it must be possible to design a *systematic theory of categories* or, even more, a theory of the possible, radically distinguished regions within being, which then would have to function as a so-to-say heading for the ordered sequence of *a priori* disciplines to be systematically worked out in the future. It was evident to me from the outset that in this all that is phenomenologically *a priori* must be contrasted with the remaining and, in an essential sense, *ontologically a priori*. Even if in the end, it became apparent to me that all cognition of essence has likewise an essential *connection* [*Wesenszusammenhang*], I

cannot view as a step forward much less a discovery[41] the step
which, a number of years after the publication of my "Prolegomena," attempted to go beyond my *a priori* theory of objects as
such by introducing the *term* "theory of objects" as a title for the
completely vague collection of all "homeless" objects. I see myself compelled to oppose strongly the, in my opinion, confused
‹323› and often contradictory ideas of Meinong's[42] theory of objects (a
theory which would not be so vague and contradictory if its
founder himself had conducted even one piece of theory of objects
investigation or had himself studied better the *Logical Investigations*, which had been available for a long time) because in the
more recent literature the investigations of Meinong and myself
are constantly cited as if they ran parallel to and supplemented
each other systematically — something which, according to my
observations, must produce misinterpreting prejudices in those
who do not yet know my work.

Section 8. *Critical Differentiation from Lotze.*

The fact that the present *Investigations* have picked up strong
and gratefully recognized inspiration from the writings of Lotze
and Bolzano has likewise given rise to misinterpretations which
frequently stand in the way of the understanding of the true
meaning of the epistemology breaking through in them (regard-

---

[41] The German text in *Tijdschrift* reads: "Stellte sich mir zum Schluss auch heraus,
dass alle Wesenserkenntnis ebenfalls einen Wesens*zusammenhang* hat, eine Reihe von
Jahren nach dem Erscheinen meiner Prolegomena, so kann ich doch den Schritt, der
über meine apriorische Theorie der Gegenstände als solcher hinaus dadurch versucht
wurde, dass man das *Wort* Gegenstandstheorie als Titel für das völlig vage Zusammen
aller "heimatlosen" Gegenstände einführte, nicht als einen Fortschritt, geschweige
denn als eine Entdecking ansehen." This makes it appear that "eine Reihe von Jahren
nach dem Erscheinen meiner Prolegomena" modifies "stellte sich mir zum Schluss
heraus" — i.e., "even if in the end, a number of years after the publication of my
Prolegomena, it became apparent . . ." There seems to be a transcription error here,
however, since the original 1913 manuscript reads: ". . . Wesenszusammenhang hat,
so kann ich doch den Schritt, der eine Reihe von Jahren nach dem Erscheinen meiner
Prolegomena über meine apriorische Theorie . . ." We have translated it this way
since it makes better sense in light of the historical facts: it was several years after
Husserl's publication of the "Prolegomena" in 1900 that Meinong published his
Untersuchungen zur Gegenstandstheorie (1904) [Trans. note].

[42] Alexius Meinong (1853–1921) was a German philosopher who, like Husserl, had
studied under Brentano. Most of his work was in the area of philosophical psychology
although his early epistemological theories (especially the "theory of objects" here
referred to) also exercised considerable influence at that time. Meinong's theory of
abstracting from existential claims to concentrate on the essence of objectivities is
similar in many respects to Husserl's phenomenological reduction [Trans. note].

less of whether or not one agrees with it). The manner in which I have worked over Lotze's theory of validity [*Geltung*] and his theory of ideas (which is the Platonic [theory] in the sense of his interpretation) led to epistemological trends and, in the continuation, to the actual, though as yet incomplete, development of an epistemology which is of a fundamentally different type from Lotze's epistemology — as different as, for example, the epistemology of Aristotle is from that of Plato or as the epistemology of Kant is from that of Lambert.[43]

First of all, it should be mentioned here that nearly all critics who render judgment on the present work with such relish and, for the most part, so disparagingly have contented themselves with a reading of the first volume (and usually a very superficial reading) and paged through the second volume only looking for references. But as for those who were conscientious enough to have let a study of the second volume also precede their critique, it can be proved precisely from their misinterpretations that they have read either not at all or only superficially and selectively the phenomenologically and epistemologically most important investigations — *viz.*, the fifth and, above all, the sixth. Only one who confines himself merely to the first volume and in so doing does not even think it through thoroughly could identify my anti- ‹324› psychologism, my theory of ideas and theory of knowledge (insofar as the latter can be judged at all from minor indications of it) with Lotze's or would even attempt to contrast them according to their general type.

To mention only one point: Lotze also, to be sure, fights against a founding of logic and of the logical noetic through psychology, but that does not in any way hinder us from counting him, when measured against the meaning of anti-psychologism which governs the "Prolegomena," among the adherents of psychologism, anthropologism, and naturalistic relativism — just as is similarly the case for very many authors who have of late posed as convinced opponents of psychologism. Lotze abandons the theory of ideas, seemingly presented as something so pure, in the later

---

[43] J. H. Lambert (1728–1777) was a proponent of the Leibniz-Wolffian school who attempted an eclectic reconciliation between rationalism and empiricism. He corresponded with Kant and is considered an important forerunner of Kant's critical philosophy [Trans. note].

development of his presentation. Thus, in the fourth chapter, page 155, of his *Logic*[44] of 1874 he says,

> If "a" and "b" are not, as heretofore, things of an independent reality beyond our thought but are rather conceivable characteristics like red and green, straight and crooked, then there exists a relationship among them only insofar as we think it and because we think it. But our mind is so constituted, and we so presuppose for every other whose interior resembles ours [*deren Inneres dem unseren gleicht*] that the same "a" and "b", no matter how often or by whom they are conceived, will bring about in thought the same relation which exists only through thought and only within it. And herein lies that which we mean when we consider the relationship as one that exists in-itself between "a" and "b."

Time and again the talk is of *our* thinking and, to be sure, in a genuinely anthropologistic sense. Hence, there is also for him an "abyss of wonderment" in the possibility of knowledge — the open confession of a failing epistemology. Proper epistemology clarifies, and something clarified is both something become understandable and something understood — thus the extreme opposite of "wonderment." Reference is repeatedly made to both the nature of all minds — actually understood as a fact of reality — and over against this, the nature of real things in themselves. And the completely distorted problem of the real and formal meaning of the logical comes about through the fact that Lotze <325> presupposes a metaphysical world of things that exists in-itself and, over against it — at least according to our usual knowledge-claim — a world of ideas, meant to represent these things, that belongs to minds existing in the [metaphysical] world, and that he understandably now struggles in vain to explain the basis of the correspondence between these two worlds within knowledge.

Lotze does not see the *real* problem of an epistemological elucidation of knowledge — a problem which is in our sense that of the phenomenological clarification of its essence and, correlatively, the eidetic problem of a knowable world as such. He does not see the absurdity that lies first in finding the *possibility* of knowledge in general (and specifically knowledge of the real) to be in principle enigmatic and then, in the solution to this enigma, in making supposedly obvious presuppositions which themselves are part of

---

[44] The original 1913 manuscript reads "page 555f." [Trans. note].

the enigma. But precisely this is what Lotze does in the most diverse expressions. Such a presupposition is the *thinkability* of a reality "in itself" which has nothing to do with any of our cognitions or forms of cognition but which our cognitions, our representations [*Vorstellungen*], and our modes of representation [*Vorstellungsweisen*] are eventually somehow supposed to approach and to grasp. Another such presupposition with Lotze[45] is a mythological metaphysic: he distinguishes a representational world [*Vorstellungswelt*] which has merely human-subjective validity from a metaphysical world of monads in-themselves concerning which, under the label of metaphysics, we can venture metaphysical proposals by completely mysterious methods. Such proposals are inferior to novels, since novels have an aesthetic truth, and hence, an essential common ground with reality that is intelligible, something which is necessarily lacking in all such metaphysical fiction.[46]

But however much Lotze's work lacks radical strength and decisiveness and, accordingly, inner conclusiveness, it is still for the epistemology of the last century one of the most significant, detailed, profound and enlightening expositions — for which, however, there was no follow-up. The present investigations owe him very much in the thinking out and thinking to conclusion [of his ideas] which brought forth in all directions novel thought-constructions both in details and as a whole. In doing this, my book does not set as its goal an elucidation of the possibility of ‹326› cognition of any sort, and certainly *not* the cognition of reality, but rather that of the possibility of *analytic* cognition, which I take to be the primary and fundamental type of cognition. This does not, of course, preclude the fact that some of the investigations concern at the same time the problems of cognition of reality.

Section 9. *Critical differentiation from Bolzano.*

With respect, on the other hand, to my alleged development of

---

[45] The German reads: "Das andere ist bei Lotze ..." which might also be rendered as "Everything else in Lotze is ..." This seems too strong for the context and, hence, we have translated it in a weak sense [Trans. note].

[46] The German text in *Tijdschrift* reads: "*Dichtungen*" (poetry) which seems to be a mistranscription of "Erdichtungen" (fiction) in the 1913 manuscript [Trans. note].

Bolzano, it need only be pointed out briefly that for Bolzano not only are the idea of a *mathesis universalis*, and moreover, the idea of a pure theory of forms of meaning and the other ontological expositions of these volumes totally foreign to him but, with respect to what he had to offer me as valuable, also the entire *idealistic* intent which belongs essentially to my idea of pure logic remained foreign to him. Bolzano's propositions, ideas, and truths "in themselves" are anything but the meanings of "ideal" unities. He would have firmly rejected the idea of a pure logic in my sense — and, even more, in the sense of a pure logic "to be clarified" epistemologically. One must not judge without a more exact knowledge of Bolzano's work; one must not read superficially or look around in Bolzano for quotations in order to attribute my thoughts to specific like-sounding propositions in his work. No one has taken notice of the fact that Bolzano's epistemology rests upon the foundation of an extreme empiricism. Thus, he says of logic, arithmetic, geometry, and pure physics:

> ... that these disciplines enjoy so great a certainty only because they have the advantage, that the most important of their theories can be themselves very easily and in various ways verified through experience ... We are so certain of the correctness of the rules "Barbara," "Celarent," etc.[47] only because thousands of tests in our conclusions which we carried out according to them certify them." "As long as we have not convinced ourselves of the correctness of a proposition either by experiment or by repeated testing of its method of derivation, we do not yet, if we are at all smart, grant it any unconditional trust in spite of all that critical philosophy might recite to us about the infallibility of the pure intuitions upon which our judgment here is supposed to be based. (*Wissenschaftslehre III*, pp. 244f.).

<327>

Therefore, there is here no difference between Bolzano and his contemporary, John Stuart Mill. It is no less puzzling when one names Bolzano as the founder of phenomenology; Bolzano, who, to be sure, like countless others, occasionally makes good, sometimes even phenomenologically usable remarks, but who was removed from phenomenology by veritable abysses of [mis-]understanding and certainly incomparably farther removed [from phenomenology] than either Hume or Mill. His genius lay in a mathematical method of examining logical matters that could not be misled by the prejudices of any school; it is a thoroughly naive

---

[47] "Barbara" and "Celarent" are labels for the first two models — "AAA" and "EAE" — of valid syllogistic forms [Trans. note].

method of examination, as naive as that which mathematicians practice in their number theories or in their theories of geometrical magnitudes. But what he did see, he did not let himself be talked out of (at least to a large extent) — and he saw a lot. To characterize him as a "scholastic logician" is to disparage both him and good scholasticism without knowing what one is talking about; and I must consider it unjust when Windelband[48] labels him an "insignificant ponderer." He was[49] the very opposite of a ponderer; his clear and sober vision hit upon things which he knew how to masterfully comprehend and to evaluate. Real treasures lie hidden in his original theory of syllogisms and in his beginnings at a scientific theory of probability; one has only really to study them — and in the sense that one studies doctrines in arithmetic. Even if he, guided by certain prejudices, both reinterprets the actually occurring and original modes of inference and also substitutes equivalent ones for them, there still lie great and unrealized values hidden in these reinterpretations as equivalents. But he has done little to elucidate logical thinking. He, just like all his contemporaries, did not anticipate the immense problems in the theory of meaning and in the theory (which is essentially related to the theory of meaning) of a categorial consciousness in its various formations. Neither did he sense in any way the truly immense complex of research investigations — which I include together under the title "phenomenology" (that is, to be sure, "pure" phenomenology). In this respect not even the faintest ‹328› beginnings are to be found with him.

Section 10. *Repudiation of the slogan: "Phenomenology as the analysis of the meanings of words."*

I shall attack right here the discussion of yet another misunderstanding that is again hard to comprehend — hard to comprehend for anyone who knows the present work in its context. It appears to have become almost a slogan (especially since it has entered into the accounts intended for beginners) that phenomenology is nothing more than "analysis of meanings" — i.e., analysis of that which is meant by concept or judgment or, as the

[48] Wilhelm Windelband (1848–1915) was a German philosopher who was and still is primarily known as an outstanding historian of philosophy. [Trans. note].
[49] Reading "war" for "was" [Trans. note].

author of a recently published book says in unsurpassible scrupulousness, it is "a somewhat differentiated analysis of the meanings of words."

To be sure, the investigations of the second volume occupy themselves to a great extent with meanings. But to say that phenomenology is a theory of meaning or, even more concretely, that it is a certain analysis of the essence of meanings — that would be as if one had said at the time of the beginnings of infinitesimal calculus that this discipline was a theory concerning the problem of tangents. And again with the same right one could say that geometry was the science of straight lines and triangles. The second volume does not pretend to be an account of phenomenology nor a text composed with the intention of grounding a phenomenology, but rather it presents itself as a series of "preliminary investigations," which the author had deemed as indispensable in the interest of an epistemological "elucidation" of the *mathesis universalis*. And since the logical element in logical phenomena is given to consciousness and since the logical phenomena are phenomena of predicating and thus of a certain signifying [*Bedeuten*], the investigation begins after all with an analysis of these phenomena. Whoever has read only the introduction (to the first edition) and then some sizeable portions of the work must surely over and over again have hit upon the fact that phenomenology is spoken of in an incomparably broader area, that analyses are <329> carried out on perception, fantasy, pictorial-representation [*Abbildvorstellung*] and thus on many sorts of experience-types that occasionally occur in connection with verbal phenomena and that occur especially where these phenomena are to become logical cognitions supplying evidence but for which this connection with the *Logos* is entirely extra-essential. What is also brought into this [investigation] are phenomenological analyses not only of objectifying acts but also of non-objectifying acts — in short, of all kinds of "experiences" or phenomena that also allow an immanent *psychological* description; [it is] only that the phenomenological approach is one that is in a certain way basically altered.

Section 11. *A misunderstanding of the author's in the* Logical Investigations. *The misleading characterization of phenomenology as descriptive psychology.*

Serious deficiencies in the first edition are connected with the fact that I had to publish the work before the insights I had won had been fully intrinsically consolidated or before I could manipulate them with complete freedom. The different sections developed at different times, and a final reworking was necessary to bring everything into a single standpoint. Because of inner uncertainty, however, during the final composition, I either fell back repeatedly into the old habits of thought or was incapable of carrying through everywhere the distinctions I had already recognized in one context as necessary. In particular, this also holds true of the *relationship between descriptive psychology and phenomenology.*

De facto the analyses were carried out as *analyses of essences* but not everywhere in an equally clear, reflective consciousness. The entire refutation of psychologism is based on the fact that the analyses (especially those of the sixth investigation but also the others) are claimed to be analyses of essences, hence apodictically evident analyses of ideas. In general, however, I did not want to concede to myself that what I for many years had looked upon as far as psychology was concerned as derived from inner "adequate perception" should now all be *a priori*, or, be comprehensible as <330> such. The wavering and misleading "Introduction" has certainly taken its toll in the effects of the work, and I felt the defect very soon after the publication of the work. With this defect went also the insufficient emphasis on the exclusion of all empirically reality-oriented (and, in the normal sense, psychological) anticipations and existential postulations. A statement in the annual report on logic in the *Archiv für [systematische] Philosophie* of 1903 brought significant improvements in that the misleading and (if understood naturally) completely *incorrect* characterization of phenomenology as descriptive psychology was decisively ruled out by means of the sharp emphasis upon the exclusion of psychological apperception (that is, of all conceptualization of experiences as conditions of real mental beings and, together with this, of all predications about reality in this sense) and "by means of" the emphasis on "intuitive abstraction." I would have done well sometime to have spoken a little more thoroughly on this point and to have expressed definitely (as I have done from the very beginning in my Göttingen lectures)[50] that all phenomenological analyses of any kind, wherever they make general observations (on perception in general, on memory, on imagination in general, or on psychological perception in general, etc.) have the character of *a priori* analyses in the only valuable sense of analyses that subject ideas given in pure intuition (i.e., self-given in genuinely original intuitive experience) to a pure description of their essential content. In the meantime my comprehensive presentations in the *Ideas*[51] have appeared which deal with the meaning and method of phenomenology on a considerably higher level of insight and with thoroughly researched horizons that I did not yet have at my disposal in 1900. It is thus a misunderstanding for which I myself am responsible to view phenomenology as a merely descriptive psychology, although some careful readers of the work (and specifically those of the younger generation) have, independently of my teaching, understood its full meaning by taking their cue from the sixth investigation.

<331> Section 12. *The charge of "logicism"; critical discussion on Wilhelm Wundt.*

This is the place to deal with the strange reproach for "logicism" which has so often been made against the present work. No less a person than *Wilhelm Wundt*[52] found it necessary to publish in 1910 a great and truly brilliant essay (in the first volume of his *Kleinen Schriften*) under the title *Psychologismus und Logizismus [Psychologism and Logicism]*, whose main theme is to show the complete wrongheadedness of logicism. But at the same time the

[50] Cf. *The Idea of Phenomenology* (The Hague: Martinus Nijhoff, 1964) for an example of Husserl's Göttingen lectures on this topic [Trans. note].

[51] *Ideas: A General Introduction to Phenomenology*; Edmund Husserl; trans. by Boyce Gibson; New York: Macmillan, 1931 [Trans. note].

[52] Wilhelm Wundt (1832–1920) was a German philosopher who is best known for his work in physiology and psychology. He is one of the men accredited with establishing psychology as an independent science [i.e., distinguishing it from both philosophy and physiology]. He set up the first laboratory for experimental psychology in Leipzig in 1879. As a student of mathematics in Leipzig in 1876/77, Husserl attended Wundt's philosophy lectures but they do not seem to have impressed him much at that time [Trans. note].

essay is concerned also with logicism's historical necessity as the
final and most radical intensification of the age-old deceptive
motifs which recur in the course of history in ever new dialectical
disguises, which have essentially determined the historical typol-
ogy of the scientific augmentation of psychology and logic, and
which have only now lived themselves out in the *Logical Investigations*. The culminating intensification means *eo ipso* its scientific and historical overcoming.[53] Now, and especially following
Wundt's argumentations, the unsurpassible absurdity of logicism
must be evident to everyone; everyone must resolve to radically
eliminate the logistical tendencies which are operative in oneself
from deep psychological sources. Wundt carried out his investigations on psychologism and logicism in a parallel fashion. Psychologism is for Wundt — whom we had heretofore all viewed as
the greatest adherent of psychologism — a parallel absurdity.
And the truth lies, according to Wundt, I do not want to say in
the middle but rather somewhere else. I apologize for this vague
way of putting it, since the famous researcher has not expressed
himself on this in a manner comprehensible to me. Unmistakably
the expositions on psychologism are in interest and intellectual
force far inferior to the historical-critical treatment of logicism,
whose refutation is, as one soon sees, close to the author's heart
or, as I already have said, the true theme of the essay.[54]   <332>

Wundt defines logicism as the attempt, using the paths of
logical reflection, to account for the relationship among appearances — and especially among those which are given to us in our
own consciousness. The real sense of this definition will become
clearer if I turn now to the interpretations which he has carried
out on my work.

Let us disregard at present the first volume, of whose critique
of psychologism Wundt essentially approves, and turn immediately to the second, the importance of which he recognized at once as
exceeding that of the first volume. He treats it in a two-fold
context: once from the viewpoint of the establishment of an
extremely logistic psychology, and the other from that of laying
the phenomenological foundations for a pure logic. The distinction

[53] Reading "wissenschaftliche" for "wissenschaftlich" [Trans. note].

[54] Here approximately two printed pages of sharp polemic against W. Wundt
which, however, have no relevant interest, have been deleted by the editor [Fink's
note].

is important and due to extra ordinarily deep insight. Except for
Wundt, only Dilthey[55] from among the older generation of
scholars recognized the import for psychology of the investigations
of the second volume, and, aside from a few younger researchers
who were influenced early by these two, this relationship has remained unnoticed. I myself did not say a word in this work about
a reform of psychology and did not express my conviction until
my article in *Logos* (1911)[56] to which the anticipated response was
not lacking. Wundt thus saw psychology, the foremost field of his
life's work, threatened, and his primary and most important
interest was to rescue it from the misuses of logicism, from the
"invasion of logic." For, as he laments, "we stand today unmistakably under the sign of logicism" (p. 521). This latter point
I consider, of course, a great misunderstanding. But it is true that
we are engaged in a great reorientation in psychology. And even
if the volume of the *Logical Investigations* under examination has
not a single programmatic word to say in this regard but rather
directly attacks some of the fundamental problems related to
logical thinking and its correlates and provides pieces of developing work, it is indeed unmistakeable that what is done there also
<333> essentially concerns psychology and, if correct, prepares new
methods for dealing with psychological problems, and thus really,
as Wundt says, implies a "reform of psychology." I know that I
must thank Wundt very much that he did not pass over this with
a smile, as did so many, but rather that he took it seriously — no
matter what stance he may have taken later on.

Likewise, he notices, though dimly, connections with rationalism and apriorism of older periods, although the meaning of a
theory of essences for phenomena could not, obviously, dawn
upon him since it had even remained completely hidden from him
both that my method was a strictly "intuitive" one — i.e., a
radical method of intuitive experience in my expanded sense —
and also that precisely therein lay the unfathomable difference

---

[55] Wilhelm Dilthey (1833–1911) was a German philosopher best known as the
founder of *"Lebensphilosophie"* [Life philosophy]. Most of his important work is in
history of ideas; his theory of "world views" [*Weltanschauung*] provided a new methodological basis for a humanistic study of culture and society. Husserl carried on a
correspondence with Dilthey for some time after the publication of the *Logical
Investigations* and held him in high regard [Trans. note].

[56] "Philosophy as Rigorous Science"; cf. *Phenomenology and the Crisis of Philosophy*
(New York: Harper and Row, 1965), pp. 71-148 [Trans. note].

between my rationalism and idealism as compared with previous types, let alone as compared with all scholastic ontologies. Thus, the decisive point in Wundt's misunderstandings as well as of all similarly oriented contemporaries is already characterized. He labels and interprets my work as "logicism." Evidently referring to this, he speaks of an invasion of logic and conceives it as the culmination of the ever-repeated attempts "to achieve an understanding of positive life by somehow interpreting it logically or by resolving it into dialectical constructions of concepts." He speaks of the aspiration to crown the work of logic by ultimately, after it has annexed knowledge in its farthest reaches to its domain, having also the phenomena of subjective consciousness, which seemingly defy every logical norm, subjected to its control (p. 516). He speaks of the empire-building tendencies of logical reflection — which endeavor to transform psychology itself into a minor province of general logic! On p. 519 he characterizes me directly as one "who in a ruthlessly executed logicism (shortly before this he called it scholastic logicism) tries to transform psychology itself into a reflective articulation of concepts and words." And on page 572 he speaks of "this most radical of all attempts that set out to transfer the psychical into the logical."

Whoever has not only "attentively read" my work but rather has, in a spirit of unprejudiced cooperation such as this work after all requires, actively produced the phenomena in himself and has ‹334› performed the analyses and [grasped] the meanings of the descriptions as well — such a one will hear such pronouncements only with the greatest astonishment. Of course, in logical investigations the logical is at stake in the work, and in the second volume logical phenomena are treated. Hence we start out in the first, initially empirical-psychological approach from the fact of an I think, of an I assert: "this paper is white," or I understand this sentence, I understand generally words and sentences and soon enunciate them, or I hear them, or they occur to me, they go through my head without my "asserting," really "judging," etc. Is it "scholasticism" if one once *looks at* these phenomena, if one asks about the differences between the phenomena — between phenomena that are directly graspable in immanent reflection and are distinguished according to whether "the same" judgment is performed "intuitively" or "non-intuitively" ("merely symbolic-

ally") and the like? Is it not allowed to examine, to describe generally, and to fix terminologically the phenomenon which is before me when I "verify on the basis of an intuitive experience" a non-intuitive predicative opinion and specifically a merely symbolically performed predicative judgment? Is it a fabrication when a certain relation of unity and transition, a way of association unique to it, between two lived-experiences is discovered, established purely intuitively, and if one then selects the term "fulfillment" for this? Obviously, one cannot read and understand the *Logical Investigations* in the way one does a newspaper. One can understand descriptions only if he knows that which is described, and he can only know what is described if he has brought it into clear intuitive experience. Therefore, it is this intuitive experience which demands a step-by-step presentation, the whole effort and technique of which consists precisely in directing [the reader] through the only possible means of the word to the production of intuitive experience and then in fixating this through "concepts" — concepts which cannot be and must not be anything other than pure "expressions" of the "essence" of that which is intuited. Wundt pretends to understand everything that is psychological — but unfortunately there are huge domains of
<335> experiences which he has never entered; he has never made them reflectively into an object of investigation and he has never seen entire worlds of immanent differences within them. He refuses on principle to assume the indeed extraordinary toil of reflective and, generally, phenomenological analysis. And he refuses to do this because he concludes, as the true *"a priori"* philosopher, that there cannot be such things. There is no remedy for *this* sort of apriorism. One cannot come to an understanding with someone who is both unwilling and unable to see. Seeing is not always a simple matter, not even when considering external nature. The biologist using his microscope sees very much more than the porter; he has learned a type of seeing that the latter has not learned. He cannot really demonstrate this seeing to anyone, and whoever has *a priori* arguments that rule out a certain type of seeing will never be able to be convinced even by a microscope. Granted that there are deceptions in phenomenological seeing because of interpretative projections, but are there any fewer in

the case of external seeing? Is the description of no value because there are deceptions in description?

But I need not go into method. The basic fact is that Wundt, in whose work one will hardly ever find a genuinely pure analysis of phenomena, of phenomena in their pure content, repudiates all comprehensive analyses of this type in that he does not translate them back into the intuition which he lacks and which he holds to be impossible on *a priori* grounds. For more than three decades[57] all of my work has been in the area of immanent, intuitive experience. I have learned, laboring under unprecedented difficulties, to see and to keep projections away from that which I see. I see *phenomenological differences* — especially, *differences of intentionality* — as well as I see the difference between this white and that red as pure data of color. If someone absolutely cannot see differences of the latter sort, then one would say, he is blind; if someone does not see differences of the other sort, then I cannot help saying once more, he is blind — even if it is blindness in a broadened sense. Can I allow myself to be made uncertain by the fact that Wundt concludes on *a priori* grounds by means of a highly ingenious historical construction that these differences, <336> which stand for me on the same level as the difference between red and green, are (perhaps because I used *words* to characterize them) a logicist construction, a transformation of the actual sense-data into scholastic logic, etc.?

Let the reader try just once to read every assertion which I make in phenomenological contexts just as he reads a zoological or botanical description of an object — thus as an expression standing for something intuitively experienced or intuitively experienceable and as something that is really originally understandable only through direct intuitive experience. Such an attempt is called the study of this book, and every word which is spoken about this book without this redeeming intuitive experience (and possibly without the disproving one) is just so much hot air. This is the "evidence" of "inner intuitive experience" that is required. There are, to be certain, many sources of error in spite of this evidence, that of the illicit generalization, for example, or

---

[57] In the 1913 manuscript, Husserl had written "two decades." This was apparently changed during one of the rewritings — most likely 1924 (cf. text-critical notes in translator's introduction) [Trans. note].

that of the incomplete distinction which considers two phenomenological levels that do not stand out clearly enough as being
one level, as when an explorer interprets two different rivers to be
parts of a single one even though he performs experienced observation but one that is incompletely carried to its conclusion.
This is the field of scientific verification but the verification is not
such that one denies the *only possible authority*, that of *intuitive
experience*, or tries to displace it through indirect means which
actually presuppose it. Everything that Wundt says to characterize my procedure belongs (as it must be allowed me to say without
exaggeration) to the realm of pure fantasy — as everyone who
really checks with open eyes will confirm without hesitation.
There are, then, no logical or "scholastic" fabrications, no im-
portation of randomly selected schemata, and absolutely nothing
of the apparatus of irrelevant dialectics, of the kind that precisely
Wundt employs so masterfully in order to convince himself and
his readers that all of these givens of immanent intuitive experience are truly "scholastic bases for fabrications." It is really a
hopeless effort to demonstrate dialectically that phenomenology
<337> is a dialectical construct. The entire being and life of phenomeno-
logy is nothing more than the most radical inwardness in the
description of purely intuitive givens. And if the *Logical Investigations* signify a step forward, it is first and foremost because of
the fact that, although much had been said previously about
description and although in particular instances some valuable
observations had been made, still what had been lacking before
was a radicalism in intuitings, i.e., a deep penetration into the
phenomena which was absolutely unprejudiced and thereby free
of interpretation, and which was furthermore as systematic as the
one this work provided. Also lacking was the realization that this
process of description can be fully fruitful only if it is not carried
out as an occasional thing determined by sporadic psychological
interests but rather is carried out in systematic universality and
in consistent phenomenological reduction. But with this arises the
decisive advance, the realization of phenomenology as a unique,
independent, and basically new science, as a science within the
framework of phenomenological reduction and, above all, within
the framework of the ideation which imprints upon every assertion
the genuine rational character: that of an insight into essence.

Phenomenology, which arose for me so purely from the force of the subject matters [*Sachen*] I examined, I at first interpreted as a novel form of — I shunned the ill-reputed phrase — "*rational psychology*," which stands in the same relation to empirical psychology as the pure theory of space, the pure theory of time and motion, and the *a priori* rational mechanics (unified as disciplines of a rational physics) stand to empirical physics. That this analogy also has its limits, that phenomenology can*not* be a *deductive* <338> mathematics of phenomenal configurations in the way that geometry is a deductive discipline of geometrical configurations, that it would be absurd to speak seriously of a geometry of colors, a geometry of tones,[58] or even of a geometry of acts; that is clear from the very beginning. Yet it belongs to the profoundest problems to account in principle for the grounds for this difference. Only much later (around 1908) the important insight was gained that *a distinction between transcendental phenomenology and rational psychology* has to be made which, to be sure, is of no concern for the empirical specialized work of the psychologist but which is of the greatest significance for transcendental philosophy in the genuine sense and specifically for the role of phenomenology as the true "first" philosophy. Only with this was the radical conquest of "psychologism" in its most basic and most universal form achieved.

The *Logical Investigations* signify, therefore, if I view things correctly and if my entire subsequent life's work has not been in vain, indeed a beginning or rather a breakthrough. They were not written for anyone who is satisfied with his prejudices, for anyone who already has his philosophy, his psychology, his logic, his epistemology. For such a one they are a hollow "scholastic logicism" or some other sort of "ism." They differ, however, essentially from other philosophical proposals through the fact that they have no intention of being anything more than probes which attempt to get at the primary presuppositions of the sense of the *Logos* and thereby of all science, and to clarify these presuppositions in specific analyses. The *Logical Investigations* are, by con-

---

[58] The German text in *Tijdschrift* reads "*Biogeometrie*" (biogeometry) which does not make much sense; the original 1913 manuscript reads "*Tongeometrie*" which we have translated in our text. It is most likely a transcription error that failed to be corrected due to its context — i.e., in a list of things Husserl says are absurd, which indeed a "biogeometry" would be [Trans. note].

trast, far removed from any attempt to persuade the reader, by way of some sort of dialectical tricks, to accept a philosophy that was for the author already an accepted fact.

On the contrary, I carry over explicitly to the work under consideration the demand of the "philosophical epoché," which I have made in my *Ideas*.[59] I suggest that one read, one intuit, one follow the descriptions and the comparative reflections. But during the reading, one [should] abstain both from all philosophies either acquired from others or developed by oneself as also from every judgment which is not won in its own active seeing and describing. One will then find some smaller or larger errors to correct just as a second explorer, who follows the footprints of his predecessor and sees the same objects, will consider some improvements to be necessary; and this will be all the more the case if he also takes criss-crossing paths which make available to him new aspects of the same things. Such a one, however, will also understand his predecessor's honest description in its relative correctness, even with its equally honest mistakes, and he will not <339> belittle the description: for he too is not infallible.

In that they contradict the entire meaning of my work, Wundt's objections do not lend themselves, of course, to a refutation that goes into specifics. Anyone who has once understood the *Logical Investigations* will, by comparing it with Wundt's expositions, immediately convince himself of this. Moreover, one understands already from what has been said the absurdity of the constant expectation with which Wundt approaches the text: the expectation of determining concepts, of definitions. It is no wonder that he is constantly disappointed. Does he by chance expect from a "Sven Hedin"[60] let us say, definitions of the settlements, tribes,[61] and wildernesses of Tibet? Hardly anything but descriptions. To be sure at stake are in his case descriptions which are easily understood from the sources of our everyday experiences of settlements, prairies, and the like. For such cases it [experience] has analogous observations at its disposal by means of which the new descriptions can be vividly reconstructed with suitable

---

[59] Cf. *Ideas*, p. 72 [Trans. note].

[60] Sven Hedin was a turn of the century Swedish explorer [Trans. note].

[61] The original 1913 manuscript reads: "*Steppen*" (prairies or steppes) rather than "*Stämme*" (tribes). The former is probably correct, in light of the use of "*Steppen*" in a later sentence, and the latter a transcriptional error [Trans. note].

modifications and combinations, whereas phenomenology demands a direct personal production of the pertinent phenomenon and a thematic attitude which is very difficult to attain and to maintain consistently: namely, an attitude toward the intentional [*das Intentionale*] with its completely unique intentional syntheses and its intentional implications and reflections — something for which the naturalism of the entire modern era was completely blind and Wundt no different from all the rest. It was *Franz Brentano* who first opened up the trail here — but only through his formal indication of the general descriptive uniqueness of "mental phenomena." He had never overcome the naturalistic prejudice in his psychology, and precisely because of this the unique sense of intentional analysis and the proper method of an intentional psychology remained inaccessible to him. The idea of a pure phenomenology however was completely beyond his reach.[62]

---

[62] Omitted here by the editor is another *merely* polemical passage about a page long directed against Wundt. With this the "Draft" breaks off [Fink's note].

N.E.

ECHEANCE	DATE DUE
DEFERRED - A PLUS TARD	
OCT 25 2004	

Université de Sudbury
University of Sudbury